TALKING MATTERS

A Practical Guide to Speaking and Listening

by

Deborah Catesby
Hilary Caminer

English and Communication Team,
Richmond Upon Thames College

HODDER AND STOUGHTON
LONDON SYDNEY AUCKLAND TORONTO

Catesby, Deborah
Talking matters: a practical guide to
speaking and listening.
1. Oral communication
I. Title II. Caminer, Hilary
808.5 P95

ISBN 0-340-38623-1

First published 1986
Third Impression 1988

Phototypeset by Macmillan India Ltd, Bangalore 25

Printed in Great Britain
for Hodder and Stoughton Educational
a division of Hodder and Stoughton Ltd, Mill Road
Dunton Green, Sevenoaks, Kent by
Page Bros (Norwich) Ltd

Contents

Introduction

The main aim of *Talking Matters* is to improve your skills of speaking and listening. Whether you're with friends, at work or at college you need to be able to put into words what you think and feel. This book consists of exercises which give practice in speaking for yourself. All the exercises are based on everyday events and in most cases you'll need to work in pairs, small groups or as a whole class.

The chapters follow a logical order, but exercises can be taken out of sequence. The first chapter, 'Using Your Voice', is worth going back to from time to time as the techniques it teaches are important whenever you speak. A final 'Extended Exercise' sums up most of the techniques taught in each chapter. The extended exercises can also be used for assessment. At the back of the book is a Skills List which indicates the skills taught in each exercise.

The cassette is an important feature of *Talking Matters*. It gives examples of various encounters, some of which go well. In others, a different approach, planning what to say before you speak, or another tone of voice would have improved matters. All you need to use it is an ordinary cassette recorder.

It would be helpful to tape (or video if you can) completed exercises so that you can listen to and assess what you've said and how you've said it.

This book is particularly suitable for students preparing for City and Guilds Foundation, 772, YTS, CPVE and selected RSA courses.

1

Using Your Voice

1.1 Tongue Twisters

The way you use your voice is important. If you can speak clearly, use a pleasant tone, and sound interesting, you're on your way to being successful in many of the things you have to do. However, it's all very well to say–not so easy to put into practice. You could start by working on how clearly you speak. Try some of these tongue twisters. The idea is to loosen up your tongue–just as you loosen up your body by doing exercises.

Tim, the thin twin tinsmith.

The sixth sheik's sixth sheep's sick.

Does your shirt shop stock short socks with spots?

Many an anemone sees an enemy anemone.

Black bug's blood, black bug's blood.

Tie a knapsack strap over three shy thrushes.

The sweetest girl I ever saw
Sat sipping cider through a straw.

Moses supposes his toeses are roses;
But Moses supposes erroneously:
For nobody's toeses are posies of roses
As Moses supposes his toeses to be.

My dame hath a lame tame crane,
My dame hath a crane that is lame.
Pray, gentle Jane, let my dame's tame crane
Feed and come home again.

A canner exceedingly canny,
One morning remarked to his granny,
'A canner can can
Anything that he can,
But a canner can't can a can, can he?'

If a woodchuck could chuck wood,
How much wood would a woodchuck chuck,
If a woodchuck could chuck wood?
He would chuck, he would, as much as he could,
If a woodchuck could chuck wood.

Can you imagine an imaginary menagerie manager
imagining managing an imaginary menagerie?

The Leith police dismisseth us,
I'm thankful, sir, to say;
The Leith police dismisseth us,
They thought we ought to stay.
The Leith police dismisseth us,
We both sighed sighs apiece,
And the sigh that we sighed as we said goodbye
Was the size of the Leith police.

Once an ant
Met a bat.
Said the bat
To the cat,
'Why the dog
Don't the elephant
Get the fish out of here?'

Swan swam over the sea,
Swim, swan swim!
Swan swam back again,
Well swum, swan!

A pleasant place to place a plaice is a place where a
plaice is pleased to be placed.

1.2 Shopping Lists

One of the problems with tongue twisters is separating one sound from another. This is a problem of *articulation*. To help practise your articulation, try reading out the rather strange shopping lists below. Work with a partner, and take it in turns to read out one of the shopping lists without repeating any of the items. The other person writes out the list, based on what you say.

List One

3 X marked 6cm screws
8 multiple edged hinge brackets
1 dozen Phillips screwdrivers
9 seven inch tap washers
38 three bore rabbit planes
6 dozen Class 1 eggs
3 economy size packets washing powder
11 double sided pan scrubbers
1 7oz tin tuna chunks
13 slices Hungarian salami

List Two

12 tins shredded textured vegetable protein
9 packets frozen fish fillets
16 dwarf rose trees
1 *Sea Witch* natural honey tinted rinse
7 packets henna and lemon hair restorer
11 9cm thin bore winches
65 6cm tin tacks
2 single edged bracket holders
3 anchor headed pins
1 large double grouter

You may have written down some rather peculiar answers, but they're not much more peculiar than the original lists. If you like, you could give scores for your answers. Give yourself a point for each word or number your partner got right when you were reading out the list.

1.3 The Telephonists' Alphabet

The phone makes the whole thing much more difficult because of noise on the line. Long distance operators use a system for spelling out difficult names. If, for example, they wanted to spell out the name MANDL, they'd say: MIKE, ALPHA, NOVEMBER, DELTA, LINDA.

Using this international alphabet, take it in turns to spell out the following names to your partner. Obviously you mustn't look at the book if you are the one who is taking the message.

Micallef	Meydancia	Mankiewicz
Michaelides	Merwanji	Maisonneuve
Micawber	Melypataki	
Mossodar	Mefmaix	

ALPHABETICAL CODE RECOMMENDED BY GPO, POLICE AND ARMY

A for ALPHA	N for NOVEMBER
B for BRAVO	O for OSCAR
C for CHARLIE	P for PAPPA
D for DELTA	Q for QUEBEC
E for ECHO	R for ROMEO
F for FOXTROT	S for SIERRA
G for GOLF	T for TANGO
H for HOTEL	U for UNIFORM
I for INDIA	V for VICTOR
J for JULIET	W for WHISKY
K for KILO	X for X-RAY
L for LINDA	Y for YANKEE
M for MIKE	Z for ZULU

1.4 What's Your Address?

Have you ever had to give your address to someone over the phone? Apparently simple numbers and street names can easily be misunderstood. For example, take this address:

40 Leighton Road,
LONDON NW7 2QH.

'Forty' can be heard as 'Fourteen'; 'Leighton' is often spelt 'Layton'; 'NW' can come out as 'SW' or even just 'W'. Any one of these mistakes can lead to a lost or delayed letter. How would you make this address clear when speaking on the phone? Are there any difficulties with your own address? How could you make sure that these addresses were heard correctly by the person you were speaking to?

1 60 BEAUFORT CRESCENT,
WREXHAM.
LM19 6FP

2 4 BLOEMFONTAIN AVENUE SOUTH,
HELIBORE,
NORTHANTS.
RS5 7DJ

3 11 WRIGGLESWORTH MANSIONS,
STRINGHAM AVENUE,
LONDON SE29 5 LJ

4 18 WALL STREET,
LOUGHBOROUGH.
DL17 4PR

1.5 Voice Exercises

Here are some other exercises which can help articulation:

1 Practise exaggerating the way you say words. If you do this in front of a mirror, you'll be able to see your lips move clearly. Most people lip-read a little, so it'll be easier for them to understand what you're saying if your lips move and change quite a lot when you're speaking. Work with a partner, and try holding a conversation without sound and without helpful gestures. See how well you understand one another.

2 Don't blur your consonants. It's easy to run one sound into another, particularly when you're talking quickly. Make sure that you sound P, T, D and K, particularly when they come at the end of a word. That way, you'll be sure that your words don't run into one another.

3 Vowel sounds are also important. Let the sound come out by really opening your mouth–don't keep it locked inside. Practice these sounds together: AAH; EE; OH. See how loud you can make them.

4 Practise deep regular breathing. It should help both the sound of your voice and your control over it.

1.6 'Good Afternoon, Mr Phillips'

A very important part of using your voice is making sure you can be heard clearly. But it's also important to get the right kind of feeling into the way you speak. *Tone* is going to come up a lot in this book, because tone is very important in making the difference between effective and ineffective speech. There are some examples of the different kinds of tone a receptionist might use on Tape Extract 1.

TAPE EXTRACT 1

Did you think any of the people you heard on the tape used the 'right' tone for their welcome? Sometimes a particular tone will be right for one occasion or type of place, but not for another. You wouldn't mind someone behind the bar at your local pub having a friendly chat and telling a few jokes along with some bits of gossip. But if your dentist's receptionist started telling a long series of dentist jokes and added a story about the man who fainted last week, you wouldn't be quite so happy. He or she would have set quite the wrong tone.

1.7 'Welcome To . . . '

You'll find below a list of places or situations where you would have to greet people. Work out the different kinds of things you'd say. Invent any necessary details. Think what kind of tone you'd use for each of them.

1 You're the guide for a tour of a chamber of horrors exhibition in the dungeon of your local castle.

2 You're an usher at your sister's wedding. It's your job to show guests to their places.

3 You're the organiser of a motorcross event on some nearby land. You have to find out if people are spectators or participants and direct them to the appropriate places.

4 You've been asked to look after your firm's exhibition stand during lunch hours. You are hoping to attract customers for your product. You want them to take some leaflets and pamphlets away and you need their names and addresses.

1.8 Animal Welfare Rights

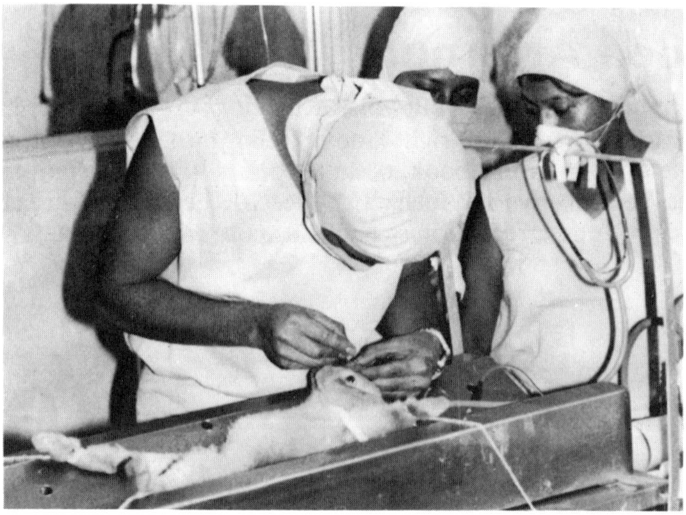

You may have heard people giving their views on radio programmes. Sometimes this happens on phone-ins, and sometimes there is a section in a programme for letters sent in by the public. You'll find below a selection of letters written after an item on Animal Welfare Rights. The programme asked for listeners' views on experiments using live animals. Practise reading out the letters in a tone of voice you think would be appropriate.

1 'I was shocked and revolted to hear that rats are being forcibly injected with substances which can cause cancer. These innocent creatures cannot protest or refuse treatment and are being forced into pain and suffering. This is a wicked and evil way to treat living creatures and I, for one, will do everything I can to stop such outrages.'

2 'As a research scientist working on a project aimed at finding cures for serious human ailments, I am somewhat surprised at the degree of hysteria provoked by our work using animal subjects. Your listeners can be assured that all possible steps are taken to make certain that no animal suffers unnecessary discomfort during the research work which is, after all, carried out for the benefit of mankind. Your listeners may one day have cause to be very grateful for the work of our laboratories.'

3 'Please, please, could you read this letter out just in case it does any good? My mother took my dog out for a walk when I was at school last week and he went off chasing ducks and got lost. We haven't been able to find him though we've offered a reward and asked anyone who might have seen him. I'm so afraid that he's been stolen by those awful people who do experiments and I must save him. He's got sort of brown and white patches over him and a brown leather collar. His name's Brownie. Why do people have to use dogs and rabbits and things for experiments? There must be other ways.'

4 'How can people believe that the lives of animals are more important than human beings? Would these protesters be prepared to offer their own bodies for vital medical experiments? There's often no other way to find cures for the terrible illnesses that afflict people. Do children have to die so that some hamster can spin round on a wheel for a little bit longer? Of course animals shouldn't be used to find new kinds of cosmetics, but it's a sin not to use them where they can help save human lives.'

If you like, you could continue the discussion, using some of the attitudes suggested by the letters, and adding any other views you have. After the discussion, think about the tones of voice you used. Were you being calm and reasonable, angry or sad or shocked? Did you *sound* the way you felt? Is it a good idea to sound the way you feel? Would your arguments have been more effective if you'd used a different tone?

1.9 Telling Jokes

If you speak clearly and use a tone which is appropriate for a particular occasion, you're already using your voice quite well. However, you'll be more effective if you can make what you say have *impact*. One way of getting impact is by pausing. If you make your listeners wait in suspense at critical moments, you'll find that they'll listen more intently to what you have to say.

Telling jokes is a good way to demonstrate this. Try telling some of these old jokes so that they have maximum impact.

Q: What did the first mind-reader say to the second mind-reader?
A: You're all right, how am I?

Q: What should you do if a child falls down a well?
A: Get a book about bringing up children.

A lady went into a pet shop. 'I want a parrot for my little girl,' she said.
'Sorry, madam,' said the shop-keeper. 'We don't do swops.'

Teacher: If you had 10p, and you asked your dad for another 10p, how much would you have?
Boy: Er, . . . 10p, sir.
Teacher: You don't know your arithmetic, boy!
Boy: You don't know my dad, sir.

A teacher was taking her class for a walk in the woods. 'Now, Mary,' she said. 'What do we call the outside of a tree?'
'I don't know, miss,' said Mary.
'Bark, you silly girl,' said the teacher, 'Bark.'
'Oh, all right then,' said Mary. 'Woof-woof!'

Patient: Doctor, doctor, I keep thinking I'm a pack of cards.
Doctor: Sit down. I'll deal with you later.

Two cats were looking at a bird in a cage. 'That's not a canary,' said the first cat, 'It's green.'
'You never know,' said the second, 'Maybe it's not ripe yet.'

You will also find that stressing significant words can bring home the real point of a joke which would be lost if you used the same emphasis for all the words. Which words would stress in the following jokes?

There was a polite family having dinner. Their little girl asked if she could leave the table and her little brother answered: 'She can't really take it with her, can she?'

Q: What's the difference between a nightwatchman and a butcher?
A: One stays awake and the other weighs a steak.

Woman: I want four nice pork chops please, and make them lean.
Butcher: Certainly, madam. Which way?

Teacher: Andy, say something beginning with 'I'
Andy: I is . . .
Teacher: No, Andy, You must say I am.
Andy: All right, I am the ninth letter of the alphabet.

First Clever Dick: Every day my dog and I go for a tramp in the woods.
Second Clever Dick: Does the dog enjoy it?
First Clever Dick: Yes, but the tramp's getting a bit fed up.

Now try telling these longer jokes so that they have as much effect on your audience as possible.

Once upon a time there was a donkey. This donkey lived in a field by the side of a river. On the other side of the river there was another field full of delicious carrots. The donkey wanted the carrots but the river was too deep for him to wade, too wide for him to swim, and there was no bridge. The donkey didn't have a boat and he couldn't fly. So how did he get across?
Do you give up?
That's all right – so did the donkey.

One day a big tortoise, a middle-sized tortoise and a little tortoise went into a cafe. They ordered three banana splits. While they were waiting, they noticed it had begun to rain.
'Look at that,' said the big tortoise, 'We should have brought our umbrella.'
'You're right,' said the middle tortoise. 'Let's send the little one back to get it.'
'I'll go,' said the little tortoise, 'Only you must promise not to eat my banana split while I'm away.'
Well, the big tortoise and the middle-sized tortoise did promise and so the little tortoise set off.
A few days later the big tortoise said to the middle tortoise, 'Come on, let's eat his banana split anyway.'
'All right then,' said the middle tortoise.
At that moment the little tortoise shouted back from the end of the cafe, 'You do that, and I won't fetch the umbrella!'

A policeman saw an old man walking towards him pulling along behind him a brick on a lead. The policeman thought, 'Poor chap's obviously daft, I'd better go and humour him.' So when the two met, the policeman said to the old man, 'Hello, I like your dog, what's his name?' The old man looked at the policeman and said, 'It's not a dog, it's a brick,' and the policeman was taken aback. 'Oh,' he said, 'I'm sorry, guv',' and he turned and walked on. The old man then looked at the brick and said, 'That fooled him, didn't it, Rover?'

1.10 Ghost Stories

Using pauses and stressing significant words can make what you say have greater impact. But there are other ways of making what you have to say sound varied and interesting. Think of some other ways and then try some story telling. Here are a couple of examples of short ghost stories. Tell them to the rest of the class in as interesting a way as you can.

Varying your *volume* is the obvious way of making a ghost story effective. If you make your voice very quiet at a critical moment you can increase the suspense, and in contrast you can make your audience jump by suddenly getting louder . . . and louder. Also, there's the business of pace – you may want suspense, but it's no good going too slowly or everyone will lose interest. You've got to speed up and slow down at the right critical moments. If you already know another ghost or horror story or can make one up, try telling it to the rest of the group.

Remember:
Pause at critical moments
Stress important words or phrases
Vary your volume
Speed up or slow down for maximum effect.

Ghost Story 1

This is a true story about events which happened about sixty years ago.

It was a beautiful summer evening just as the light was fading. A young man, my great-uncle, had been helping a friend on his farm and was cheerfully cycling home along a deserted country lane.

Suddenly in the lane immediately ahead of him he saw a young woman with a shawl over her head carrying a large bundle, which could have been a baby. He didn't know where she'd come from and she seemed not to have heard or seen him for she stood still right in his path. Terrified of hitting her, he shouted, swerved abruptly, braked and fell from his bike. Stunned and shocked, he looked up, cradling his painful arm, and expecting to find the woman just beside him. There was no one to be seen, no sound to be heard. He called out frantically, afraid of what might have happened to her, and then, when no one answered, he began a search of the hedgerows. That, too, was no use and he hobbled into the village to tell his story. His friends were amazed to find him dishevelled and almost out of his mind with fear, and though they joined in the search, nothing was ever found in the lane.

My great-uncle lived to be an old man, but he never discovered any more about the young woman he was sure he'd seen and whose image always haunted him.

Ghost Story 2

Joanne peered at the alarm clock by the bed – it was just after 2 in the morning. Downstairs in the kitchen she could hear a clanging of pans and rattle of cutlery. She couldn't understand it and was so scared that her heart beating seemed the loudest sound in the house. She shook Bob awake and they crept down the narrow stairs while the noises from the kitchen continued. Then, armed with an umbrella, they flung open the door and turned on the light.

Everything looked exactly as they'd left it the night before, except that one saucepan and a frying pan lay together in the middle of the floor. Joanne and Bob checked all round, but the back door and windows were still firmly closed. They were confused and upset – this was their first home together and they'd only been there a fortnight. They'd heard stories about the house being haunted by poltergeist, but they'd ignored such talk as sheer nonsense and superstition.

But a few nights later the nocturnal clanging in the kitchen began again. This time when they went downstairs they found some broken plates. The next time it was a smashed bottle of milk from the fridge they discovered and they became more and more frightened.

About a month after the first incident, Joanne, who could no longer sleep soundly, woke in the small hours to find all silent. She had an eerie feeling that something was very wrong. Trying to overcome her fears, she went down on her own. As she opened the kitchen door she realised with horror what had happened. GAS! She could smell gas filling the house. With her hand over her face, she flung herself at the stove and turned off the taps which were all full on. Then she pulled open the back door and gasping and choking stumbled into the garden for air.

After that Joanne and Bob decided that the poltergeist had won. They could never have felt safe again in the house, and the very next morning packed up and left. Their dream house had turned into a deadly nightmare.

1.11 Guidelines

Here are some guidelines on points to remember about using your voice.

- *articulate* clearly. It's most important that what you say can be heard. Don't slur words into one another or mumble.
- make sure that you *spell out or clarify difficult names and numbers.*
- think about what *tone* you should use for particular occasions. Should you, for example, be formal or informal, angry or reasonable, anxious or calm?
- use *pauses* to emphasise some of the things you say. Don't just run on.
- *stress* important words or phrases.
- vary your *volume*. Make your voice louder and softer at appropriate moments.
- vary your *pace*. Speed up and slow down to add interest to what you say.

Extended Exercise – Bits and Pieces

Each person in the group should prepare something to read to the others. It should be short – about one minute only – and you should spend time working on the way you are going to present it, practising stress, pausing, volume, and pace. You might decide that everyone should read something on a particular theme or subject; or it could be a free choice, reading something that you really like. You can choose a poem, a story, a fairly long joke, a speech from a play or an article from a magazine or a newspaper. It can be whatever you want, but you must try to read it so that everyone can hear and so that it has maximum impact. As you read it out, remember to look up from the page from time to time to see how your audience is reacting.

2

Instructions and Explanations

2.1 Pin Men

We give or receive instructions for many everyday tasks. Every time we buy new electrical equipment, for example, there's a set of written instructions with some diagrams attached. But we've also got to deal with oral (spoken) instructions. Here's a straightforward example: 'Take out your notebooks. Draw a couple of columns and label them **A** and **B**. Then list everything you've bought this week under **A** and what each item cost under **B**.'

But most instructions are more complicated than this. Only if they're sensibly given are they easy to understand. As you listen to Tape Extract 2 try to follow the instructions as they are given.

TAPE EXTRACT 2

The second instruction on the tape was much better because:

1 The speaker didn't hesitate or change her mind.
2 There was a clear order to the instructions.
3 She gave some helpful suggestions. For example, 'fingers like sausages'.

2.2 Draw a Picture

In pairs, and sitting back to back, each person should draw a picture or a diagram. Then take turns to give the other person instructions so that s/he can draw your diagram **using only your instructions**. Questions can only be answered with a 'yes' or 'no'. Compare the drawings. How clear were the instructions?

2.3 Bran-tub

Collect together in a box enough smallish objects to provide one for each person. The objects can be anything: tools, kitchen utensils, pieces of household equipment, car or motorbike accessories and so on. Fix up some kind of screen big enough to hide each object.

You should each take a turn at picking out an object from the box without looking. Then examine it carefully and, holding it behind the screen so that the other members of the group can't see it, you should describe what it looks like as vividly as possible. Don't mention the object's name or function, and don't use hand or arm gestures to demonstrate its shape. The rest of the group should try to draw what you describe and guess what it is. When each person has finished you should all try to assess how accurate the description was and compare the drawings with the actual objects.

2.4 A—Z: How to Get There

At some time in your life you'll almost certainly find that you have to make your way to an unknown place using only a map and perhaps some helpful suggestions. On the next two pages, you'll find a copy of the London tube map and a page from the London A–Z (scale: five inches to one mile). Work in pairs and give your partner clear directions on how to travel by tube to a convenient station and from there how to get to the destination on foot.

1 Explain how to get from Parsons Green station to the church in Byng Place (map ref. 1D).

2 Explain how to get from Lambeth North station to Great Ormond Street Hospital (map ref. 1F).

3 Explain how to get from Richmond station to the British Museum – Montague Street entrance (map ref. 2E).

4 Explain how to get from East Ham station to the National Gallery (map ref. 4D).

5 Explain how to get from Seven Sisters station to the Royal Opera House, Covent Garden (map ref. 3E).

6 Explain how to get from Pimlico station to Bow Street Police Station (map ref. 3F).

You can refer to the map and show your partner a route, but your *instructions* must be clear and to the point, giving as much help as possible. You ought to show landmarks wherever you can. Hospitals, churches, police stations, post offices etc. are marked on the map – look at the key for the symbols. The tube map shows the various lines by different types of shading. You can change tubes wherever a station shows two tube lines running through it. For example, Bond Street carries both the Central and Jubilee lines, so anyone coming from Queensway can easily change at Bond Street to get to Baker Street or anywhere else on the Jubilee line.

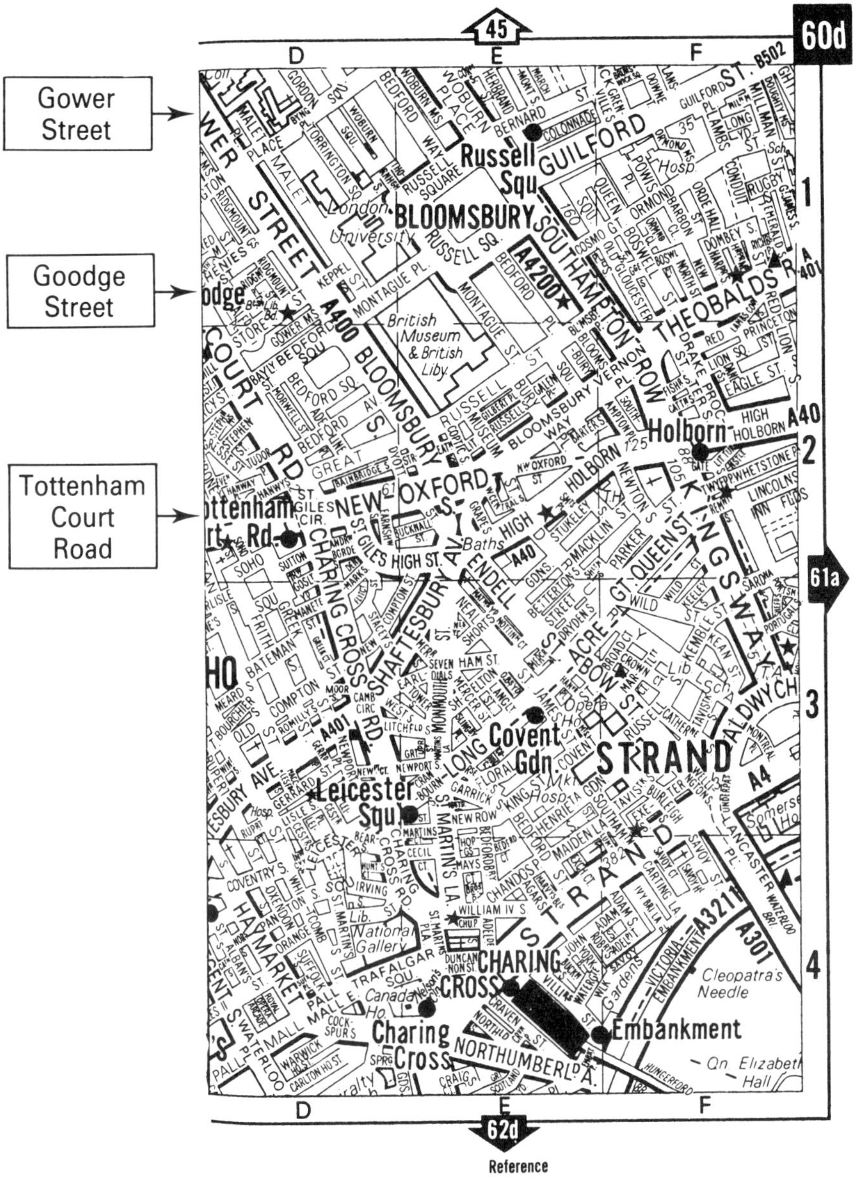

Reference

Motorway	M4
Dual Carriageway	
'A' Road	A4
'B' Road	B112
One way Streets — ONE WAY TRAFFIC FLOW IS INDICATED ON 'A' ROADS BY A HEAVY LINE ON THE DRIVERS LEFT	traffic flow
House Numbers along main roads	45
British Rail Line and Station	Selsdon
Underground Railway and Station	Leyton
Post Office	★
Police Station	▲
Fire Station	■
Hospital	Ⓗ
Information Centre	i
Place of Worship	+

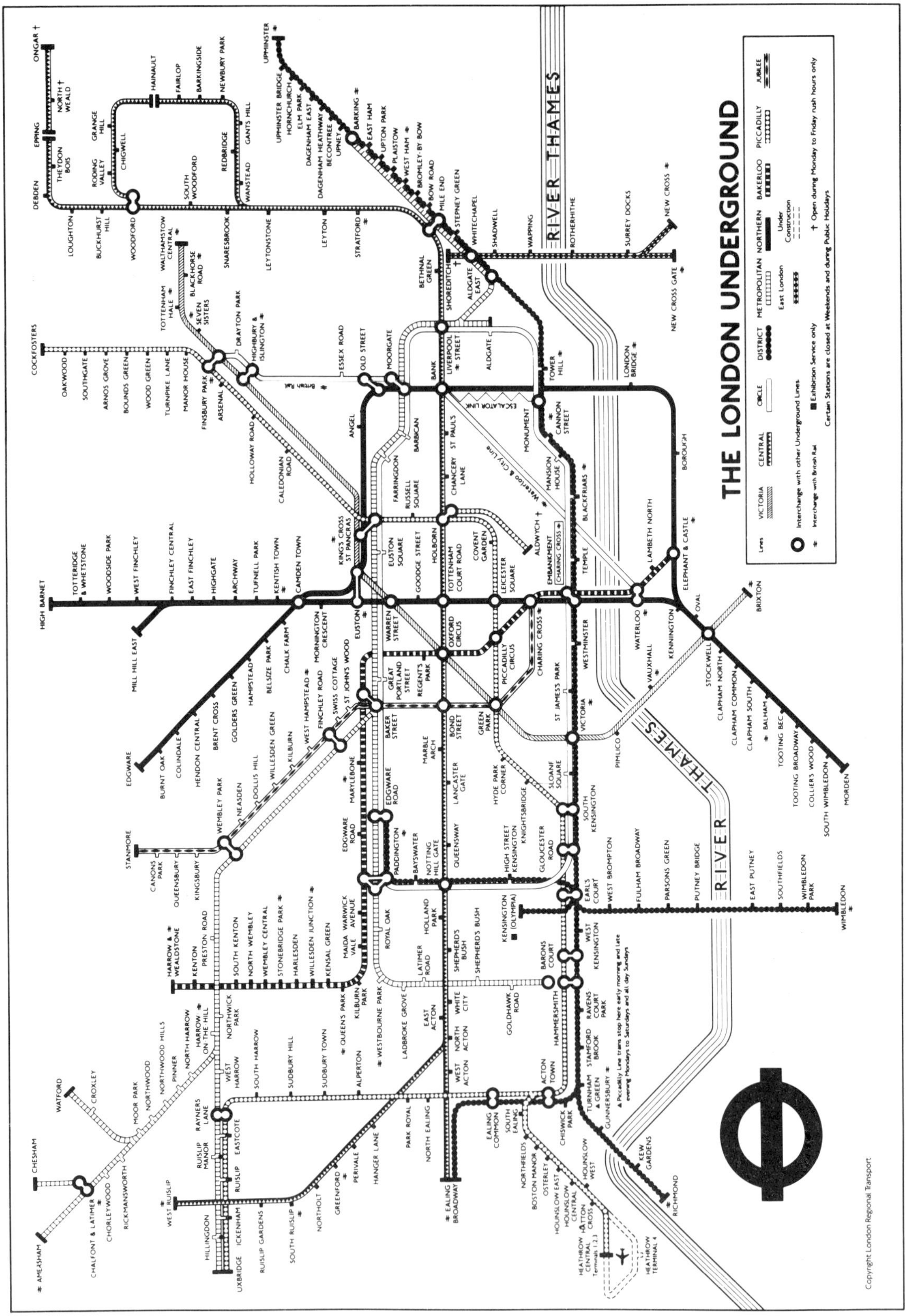
THE LONDON UNDERGROUND
Lines
VICTORIA
CENTRAL
CIRCLE
DISTRICT
METROPOLITAN
East London
NORTHERN
Under Construction
BAKERLOO
PICCADILLY
JUBILEE
Interchange with other Underground Lines
Interchange with British Rail
Exhibition Service only
† Open during Monday to Friday rush hours only
Certain Stations are closed at Weekends and during Public Holidays
RIVER THAMES
ESCALATOR LINK
Waterloo & City Line
British Rail
A Piccadilly Line train stops here early morning and late evening Mondays to Saturdays and all day Sundays
Copyright London Regional Transport
ONGAR †
NORTH WEALD †
EPPING
THEYDON BOIS
DEBDEN
LOUGHTON
BUCKHURST HILL
WOODFORD
RODING VALLEY
CHIGWELL
GRANGE HILL
HAINAULT
FAIRLOP
BARKINGSIDE
NEWBURY PARK
GANTS HILL
REDBRIDGE
WANSTEAD
SOUTH WOODFORD
SNARESBROOK
LEYTONSTONE
LEYTON
STRATFORD
UPMINSTER
UPMINSTER BRIDGE
HORNCHURCH
ELM PARK
DAGENHAM EAST
DAGENHAM HEATHWAY
BECONTREE
UPNEY
BARKING
EAST HAM
UPTON PARK
PLAISTOW
WEST HAM
BROMLEY-BY-BOW
BOW ROAD
MILE END
STEPNEY GREEN
WHITECHAPEL
SHADWELL
WAPPING
ROTHERHITHE
SURREY DOCKS
NEW CROSS
NEW CROSS GATE
BETHNAL GREEN
SHOREDITCH
ALDGATE EAST
ALDGATE
LIVERPOOL STREET
TOWER HILL
LONDON BRIDGE
WALTHAMSTOW CENTRAL
BLACKHORSE ROAD
TOTTENHAM HALE
SEVEN SISTERS
COCKFOSTERS
OAKWOOD
SOUTHGATE
ARNOS GROVE
BOUNDS GREEN
WOOD GREEN
TURNPIKE LANE
MANOR HOUSE
FINSBURY PARK
ARSENAL
DRAYTON PARK
HIGHBURY & ISLINGTON
ESSEX ROAD
OLD STREET
MOORGATE
BANK
MONUMENT
CANNON STREET
MANSION HOUSE
BLACKFRIARS
BOROUGH
HOLLOWAY ROAD
CALEDONIAN ROAD
ANGEL
BARBICAN
ST PAUL'S
FARRINGDON
RUSSELL SQUARE
CHANCERY LANE
ALDWYCH †
EMBANKMENT
CHARING CROSS
TEMPLE
LAMBETH NORTH
ELEPHANT & CASTLE
KING'S CROSS ST PANCRAS
EUSTON SQUARE
GOODGE STREET
HOLBORN
COVENT GARDEN
TOTTENHAM COURT ROAD
LEICESTER SQUARE
HIGH BARNET
TOTTERIDGE & WHETSTONE
WOODSIDE PARK
WEST FINCHLEY
FINCHLEY CENTRAL
EAST FINCHLEY
HIGHGATE
ARCHWAY
TUFNELL PARK
KENTISH TOWN
CAMDEN TOWN
MILL HILL EAST
EDGWARE
BURNT OAK
COLINDALE
HENDON CENTRAL
BRENT CROSS
GOLDERS GREEN
HAMPSTEAD
BELSIZE PARK
CHALK FARM
MORNINGTON CRESCENT
EUSTON
WARREN STREET
OXFORD CIRCUS
PICCADILLY CIRCUS
CHARING CROSS
WESTMINSTER
WATERLOO
KENNINGTON
OVAL
STOCKWELL
BRIXTON
VAUXHALL
CLAPHAM NORTH
CLAPHAM COMMON
CLAPHAM SOUTH
BALHAM
TOOTING BEC
TOOTING BROADWAY
COLLIERS WOOD
SOUTH WIMBLEDON
MORDEN
WEST HAMPSTEAD
FINCHLEY ROAD
SWISS COTTAGE
ST JOHN'S WOOD
GREAT PORTLAND STREET
REGENT'S PARK
BAKER STREET
BOND STREET
GREEN PARK
ST JAMES'S PARK
VICTORIA
PIMLICO
MARBLE ARCH
LANCASTER GATE
HYDE PARK CORNER
KNIGHTSBRIDGE
SLOANE SQUARE
SOUTH KENSINGTON
GLOUCESTER ROAD
HIGH STREET KENSINGTON
STANMORE
CANONS PARK
QUEENSBURY
KINGSBURY
WEMBLEY PARK
NEASDEN
DOLLIS HILL
WILLESDEN GREEN
KILBURN
MARYLEBONE
EDGWARE ROAD
PADDINGTON
BAYSWATER
NOTTING HILL GATE
QUEENSWAY
EARL'S COURT
WEST BROMPTON
FULHAM BROADWAY
PARSONS GREEN
PUTNEY BRIDGE
EAST PUTNEY
SOUTHFIELDS
WIMBLEDON PARK
WIMBLEDON
HARROW & WEALDSTONE
KENTON
SOUTH KENTON
NORTH WEMBLEY
WEMBLEY CENTRAL
STONEBRIDGE PARK
HARLESDEN
WILLESDEN JUNCTION
KENSAL GREEN
QUEEN'S PARK
KILBURN PARK
MAIDA VALE
WARWICK AVENUE
ROYAL OAK
WESTBOURNE PARK
LADBROKE GROVE
LATIMER ROAD
HOLLAND PARK
SHEPHERD'S BUSH
KENSINGTON (OLYMPIA)
WEST KENSINGTON
BARONS COURT
HAMMERSMITH
GOLDHAWK ROAD
WHITE CITY
EAST ACTON
NORTH ACTON
WEST ACTON
RAVENSCOURT PARK
STAMFORD BROOK
TURNHAM GREEN
GUNNERSBURY
KEW GARDENS
RICHMOND
CHISWICK PARK
ACTON TOWN
SOUTH EALING
EALING COMMON
NORTHFIELDS
BOSTON MANOR
OSTERLEY
HOUNSLOW EAST
HOUNSLOW CENTRAL
HOUNSLOW WEST
HATTON CROSS
HEATHROW CENTRAL Terminals 1, 2, 3
HEATHROW TERMINAL 4
EALING BROADWAY
NORTH EALING
PARK ROYAL
HANGER LANE
PERIVALE
GREENFORD
NORTHOLT
SOUTH RUISLIP
RUISLIP GARDENS
WEST RUISLIP
ALPERTON
SUDBURY TOWN
SUDBURY HILL
SOUTH HARROW
NORTHWICK PARK
WEST HARROW
HARROW-ON-THE-HILL
NORTH HARROW
PINNER
NORTHWOOD HILLS
NORTHWOOD
MOOR PARK
CROXLEY
WATFORD
RICKMANSWORTH
CHORLEYWOOD
CHALFONT & LATIMER
CHESHAM
AMERSHAM
RAYNERS LANE
EASTCOTE
RUISLIP MANOR
RUISLIP
ICKENHAM
HILLINGDON
UXBRIDGE

2.5 Highway Code

When you drive a car you have to follow certain rules, otherwise you can put yourself and others in serious danger. On motorways particularly, where traffic travels very fast, it's doubly important to obey the rules. But learner drivers aren't allowed on motorways, so they have to know what to do without being able to practise it. That's where instructions come in. On the next two pages you'll see the instructions on 'Lane Discipline' and 'Overtaking' reprinted from the *Highway Code*. Work in pairs, teaching each other these rules and making sure that your partner remembers them. Obviously you shouldn't just read out the *Highway Code* – put what it says into your own words.

Remember:
Order your points.
Give hints on how rules could be remembered.
Speak in a friendly way, to give your partner confidence.

After you've explained the rules on Lane Discipline, test how effective your explanation has been by asking your partner to answer the questions below:

1 On a three-lane motorway, the three lanes are the left-hand lane, the middle lane and the right-hand line. What should each lane be used for?

2 What colour are the studs on:
a) the right-hand edge of the motorway carriageway?
b) the left- hand edge?
c) between the lanes?

3 What should you do when you see a direction sign?

4 Which vehicles must not use the right-hand lane of a three-lane motorway?

Next, swap rôles so that the other partner is now the one giving the instructions, this time on 'Overtaking on the Motorway'. Test how skilful your instructions have been by asking these questions:

1 When can you overtake on the left?

2 Are you allowed to use the hard shoulder for overtaking?

3 What must you do before starting to overtake?

4 When should you be particularly careful about overtaking?

152 Even if you have missed your turn-off point or have taken the wrong route you must carry on until you reach the next exit.

153 In good visibility and weather conditions, drive at a steady cruising speed within the limits of your vehicle. You must not break the speed limits for the motorways or for your vehicle. On wet or icy roads, or in fog, keep your speed down.

154 Driving for long distances may make you feel sleepy. To help prevent this, make sure there is plenty of fresh air in your vehicle or stop at a service area, or turn off at an exit, and walk around.

Lane discipline

155 On a two-lane carriageway, drive in the left-hand lane except when overtaking.

156 On a three-lane carriageway the normal "Keep to the left" rule still applies. You may, however, stay in the middle lane when there are slower vehicles in the left-hand lane, but you should return to the left-hand lane when you have passed them. The right-hand lane is for overtaking only. If you use it, move back to the middle lane and then into the left-hand lane as soon as you can, but without cutting in.

157 To help drivers on motorways, there are amber-coloured studs marking the right-hand edge of the carriageway, red studs marking the left-hand edge and green studs separating the acceleration and deceleration lanes from the through carriageway.

158 On some motorways, direction signs may be placed over the road. Pay special attention to the signs and move into the correct lane in good time.

159 A goods vehicle with an unladen weight of more than three tons, or any vehicle drawing a trailer, must not use the right-hand lane of a three-lane carriageway unless there are exceptional circumstances.

Motorway fog

160 When driving in fog, it is vital that you should obey the rules in Rule 50.

Overtaking

161 Overtake only on the right, unless traffic is moving in

queues and the traffic queue on your right is moving more slowly than you are. Never move to a lane on your left to overtake. Never use the hard shoulder for overtaking.

162 Do not overtake unless you are sure it is safe for yourself and others. Many accidents on motorways are rear-end collisions. So before you start to overtake make sure that the lane you will be joining is clear far enough behind – use your mirror – and ahead. Remember that traffic may be coming up behind much more quickly than you think. Signal before you move out. Be particularly careful at dusk, in the dark and in fog or mist, when it is more difficult to judge speed and distance.

Remember: **Mirror–Signal – Manoeuvre.**

163 Get back to the left-hand lane or, if this is occupied, the middle lane as soon as you can after overtaking, but do not cut in on the vehicle you have just overtaken.

Breakdowns

164 If you have a breakdown, get your vehicle off the carriageway on to the hard shoulder so that it does not get in the way of other traffic. Never forget the danger from passing traffic, so do not step on to the carriageway

2.6 Darts

When you have to explain something, it's very helpful to be able to use diagrams, props or visual aids of some kind. For example, it's a lot easier to explain how to mend a bicycle puncture if you've got a bicycle wheel handy. Below, you'll see a picture of a dartboard, with a rather muddled set of instructions on how to play the game underneath. What you have to do is to explain to a beginner how to play darts. Prepare an explanation for the rest of the group, using diagrams and props to help you. You could perhaps find a real dartboard and some darts and actually demonstrate how the game is played.

Rules for Darts

Inner ring = treble
Allow the dart to float from your hand
Use three darts at a time
Score by taking away from 501 or 301
Outer ring = double
Stand ten feet from the board
Bullseye = 25 (outer ring) and 50 (inner ring)
Aim to score 501 or 301
You must start and end on a double
You must score exactly 501 or 301
If you go over the limit, simply cancel the score of the last dart thrown; that's then the end of your turn

2.7 Skills Exchange

Most people know how to do something which is a mystery to many others. For example how to iron a shirt, change a car wheel, administer first aid in an accident, or wrap up a parcel. Using diagrams and/or props if appropriate, each person should prepare a ten or fifteen minute demonstration for the rest of the class. You'll need to spend part of your time testing whether the others have understood your explanation. Don't just write down your instructions and then read them out; it's much more effective to use brief notes to jog your memory. Use the handwritten ones given below as an example:

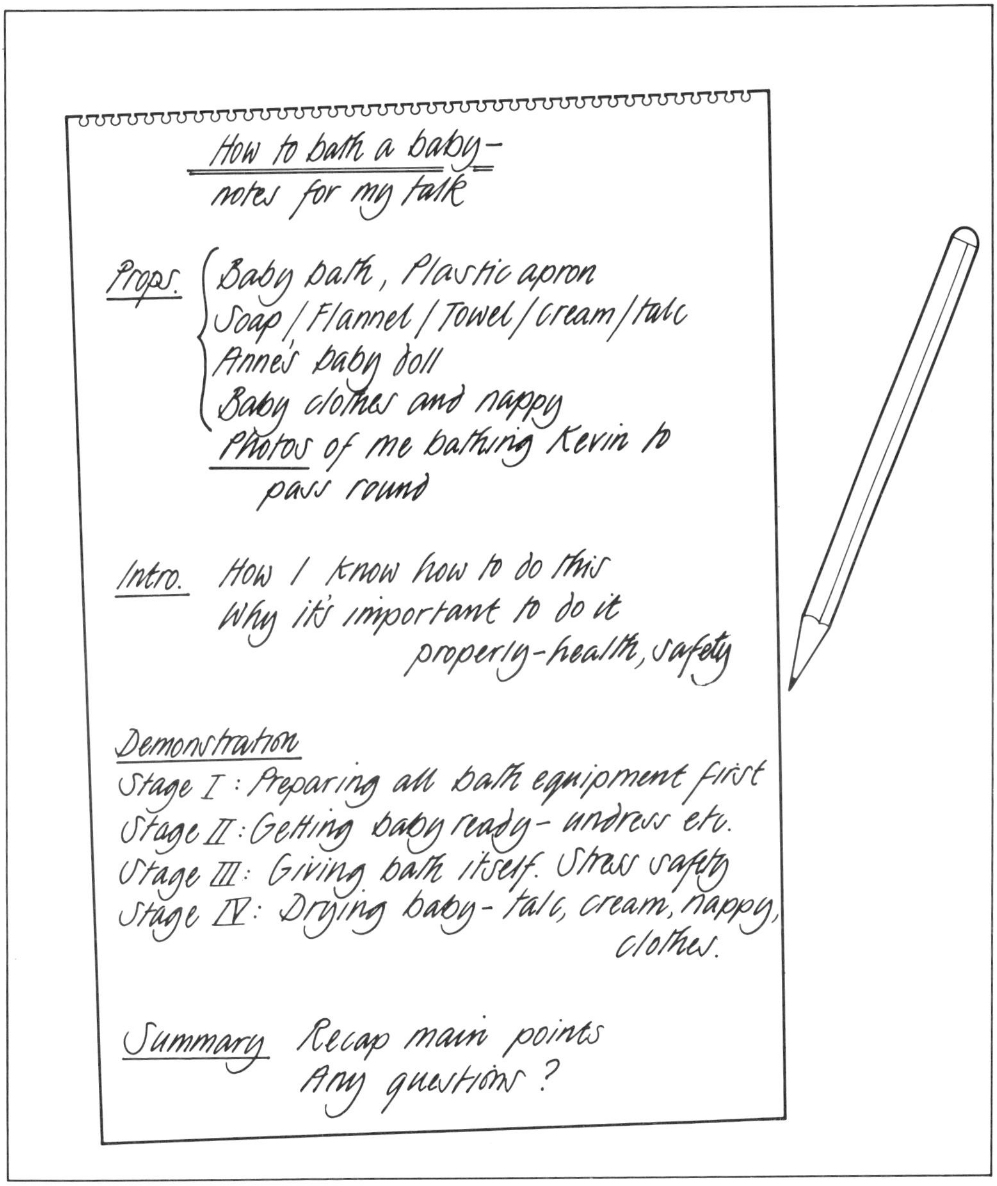

2.8 Painting Your Face

Making-up is easy for some people, but for others it's not so straightforward. What's the right way to put on eyeliner? How do you use a lipbrush? Where should you highlight the cheeks? What are the best colours to use for fair or dark skin? What do you do if you wear glasses? How do you braid your hair? And so on. Working with a partner, explain to him or her how to make up for a fancy dress party (e.g. as a clown); for a part in a play (e.g. as a very old person); or just for an ordinary day. If you can get hold of some ordinary or stage make-up it will obviously be a big help.

2.9 Back Exercises

You will see below a list of instructions on how to lift, bend or carry without straining your back. Using both talk and actions, demonstrate to a partner or small group how to follow the instructions.

1 Bend down into a squat whenever you need to reach down, for example when lifting something heavy from a low cupboard or drawer, or when gardening.

2 Stand close to any object to be lifted, positioning yourself round it if possible, with one foot forward and one back to give you a broader, more stable base to work on.

3 As you lift, bring the weight in close to you.

4 Never pick up something with your body in a twisted position.

5 Whenever you stretch upwards, tuck your bottom in and clench your lower stomach muscles before raising your arms. This prevents your lower back from arching.

6 Avoid lifting heavy weights high or lifting them down from a great height.

7 When carrying children, change sides often, and try not to twist your body as you hold them.

8 If you have to carry heavy bags, distribute the weight evenly on each side of you, and remember to stand up straight.

(Incidentally, these instructions were written originally for pregnant women, but are sensible ideas for most people.)

2.10 Guidelines

Here are some guidelines to sum up what we've covered on instructions and explanations:

- *be clear and definite* about what has to be done.
- give your instructions in a *sensible and logical order.*
- try to be helpful by *using landmarks or comparisons* to help people remember.
- use *diagrams, real objects or visual aids* whenever possible
- think carefully about whom you're speaking to and *make your instructions suitable* for them.

Extended Exercise – Radio Magazine Programme

If you listen to Tape Extract 3, you'll hear an example of part of a radio magazine programme. The presenter has asked a well-known cook to show her how to prepare a dish for a boating picnic.

TAPE EXTRACT 3

That wasn't quite as much of a disaster as it sounded. It was at least lively radio. However, the aim in this exercise is to produce an interesting programme without too much going wrong.

You should work in small groups of four or five. Each group should aim to produce two items for a radio programme which sets out to tell listeners how to perform some simple tasks. There are several suggestions given below, but you may add anything else you consider suitable, including any of the exercises from earlier in this chapter. The radio programme aims to be entertaining as well as informative, so some humour would probably help.

Suggested items

How to build a bookshelf
How to play hopscotch
How to boil an egg
How to play a scale on a piano (or small synthesizer)
How to make a child's soft toy
How to mend a bicycle puncture
How to sew on a button
How to change an electric plug
How to clean out a pet's cage or fish tank

Each group should have a producer who should follow the guidelines given below.

Producer's Guidelines

1 Before you start, think how you can make your item interesting. Think about using the following:

a) *Sound effects* – these show that what is being described actually is going on in the studio; you have to help the listeners' imagination. Examples are chopping, sizzling or stirring sounds in cookery.

b) Make sure that your presenters are actually *doing* what they're talking about within reason and commenting as they go along. Even though this is radio your listener is more likely to be interested if s/he hears real sounds of what you're doing.

2 The instructions given must be clear as well as interesting. Remember:

— be clear and definite.
— use a sensible and logical order.
— use comparisons and landmarks to help people remember.

3 Put yourself in the listener's place and consider the following questions:

a) Is this taking too long; am I getting bored?
b) Is this clear? Are the presenters taking into account that I am not an expert?
c) Can I hear properly? Are people speaking too quietly or quickly or indistinctly? Are the sound effects interfering with the explanation?

3

Listening

3.1 Hearing and Listening

What is the difference between hearing and listening? Often, even when you can hear what someone's saying quite easily because they're speaking loudly and clearly enough, you can't remember later what it was they were talking about. This is probably because it wasn't very interesting to you and you didn't concentrate. At other times, when you *are* interested in what's being said, you can often remember a lot of complicated detail. So one of the ways to listen effectively is to try to be interested in what is being said. If this doesn't work, then *focussing* your listening is another way of achieving the same thing. Concentrate on listening out for the answers to some upspoken questions, 'What is this about?' is a simple example.

There are two main kinds of listening. The first is listening for facts, and the second is listening for tone.

3.2 Chinese Whispers

This is an old game which is useful for demonstrating some of the difficulties of listening.

Form groups of seven or eight. One person in each group should think of a story, perphaps something like this:
'A man was walking along a yellow brick road. He saw a sign which pointed in three directions: South, North and West. He decided to go West. Then he climbed a steep hill, ran through a wood and finally reached a broad river.'

Don't use this example, but make notes of your own story so that you can see how carefully people have listened at the end of the game. When you've noted it down, whisper it into the ear of the person next to you. Then he or she whispers it to the next person and so on until you get to the last person who then gives his or her version of the story. Finally, read out your original version. The group whose final story comes closest to the original, wins.

3.3 Elvis

Next, listen to Tape Extract 4, which gives a short biography of Elvis Presley. Then answer the questions given below – obviously you shouldn't make notes as you listen.

TAPE EXTRACT 4

Questions

1 Where was Elvis born and on what date?
2 Which recording company did Elvis first go to?
3 What was the name of Elvis's first record?
4 Give the names of the first three songs that Elvis sang for RCA.
5 Give the names of two Elvis movies.

3.4 Digging for Facts

The next tape extract is harder, first because there are no questions to help, and second because you have to listen to some rather vague talk about the experience of gardening. However, there are four pieces of practical advice 'buried' in the extract. Listen to Tape Extract 5 and try to pick them out.

TAPE EXTRACT 5

3.5 Tiny, Tumbledown, Overpriced & Co.

One of the things that helps when listening is to be interested in what is being said. Another is to have a list of questions to guide your listening. Questions help you to pick out the relevant information from the irrelevant. So before you start listening to what someone says, be clear about what you want to know.

You'll see printed below a copy of a requirements sheet which has to be filled out for every customer who comes into an estate agent's. It's important to find out from people who want to buy a house or flat exactly what it is they want so that you don't waste time giving them irrelevant details. Listen to Tape Extract 6, which is in two parts. Fill out a copy of the requirements form for each of the two customers.

REQUIREMENTS FORM

'TINY, TUMBLEDOWN, OVERPRICED & CO.'

NAME ....

ADDRESS ....

HOME PHONE .... WORK PHONE NO:................

MAX. PRICE ....

HOUSE OR FLAT..

NO. OF BEDROOMS:..

GARDEN:..

OLDER OR MODERN STYLE PROPERTY ....

OTHER COMMENTS:..

TAPE EXTRACT 6

You probably managed to fill out the requirements form correctly in both cases. However, you'll have noticed that the more successful listening was done by the second estate agent. She came out with the opportunity to sell a good property *for* Mr Gill as well as the possibility of selling a flat *to* him. The first agent came out with nothing except a completed form. He was only interested in his form, he didn't want to listen to anything else. The second agent didn't waste time, but still succeeded in making Mr Gill feel relaxed.

Listen to the second part of Extract 6 again, and then discuss how the agent managed to make Mr Gill feel at ease and ready to trust her.

This exercise is about listening for tone as well as for facts.

3.6 Listening for Tone: Angry, Sad, Happy, Sarcastic . . .

What is tone? There's a lot about tone in this book, because getting the right tone can make such a huge difference in any spoken exchange. To take a very obvious example: if you're trying to get a bank manager to lend you £2000, you don't barge into his or her office and demand at the top of your voice to be given £2000 immediately. That's setting the wrong tone. Similarly, when you listen to someone, it's important both to get your own tone right (like the second estate agent in Tape Extract 6) and to listen to the other person's tone. Are they worried, angry, ill at ease, suspicious, sarcastic, or even helpful? If you can correctly identify their tone, the chances are you'll get on better with them.

Listen to Tape Extract 7, which consists of a series of statements made in different tones. After each one, make a note of whether you think the tone was angry, sad, happy, sarcastic and so on.

TAPE EXTRACT 7

The last example on the tape was an interesting mixture of fear and anger, which is quite a common combination. What would be the best way of dealing with that reaction? To be angry back? Or would that only cause more trouble? Once you've listened and heard that tone of fear and anger, you can deal with it much more efficiently. First of all, you can reassure the person, ignoring the anger completely. If you do that, then the chances are that the angry tone will vanish.

3.7 Body Language

So far, we've concentrated only on listening to the tone of what someone *says*. But tone doesn't only come from the voice. It also comes from the expression on people's faces, the way they hold their bodies, the emphasis they add with their hand and arm movements.

Look at the photos above and try to work out what feeling each one represents.

Working with a partner, try out on each other some of the expressions listed below. What feelings do you think each of them suggests?

1 Raised eyebrows and widened eyes.

2 Shoulders shrugged with hands held apart and open.

3 Clenched fists, bared teeth, corners of the mouth turned down.

4 Wide smile, mouth open, arms stretched out.

5 One eyebrow up, slight crease in forehead, head slightly on one side.

6 Sitting straight-backed, legs crossed, head slightly on one side, eyes looking straight at the person in front of you.

7 Shoulders slumped forward, corners of the mouth turned down.

8 Head jutting forward, lower lip stuck out, eyebrows raised, shoulders shrugging.

9 Walking with head bent down and shoulders hunched, feet dragging on the ground.

10 Biting bottom lip, clenching fists, blinking rapidly, body crouched.

3.8 Declan's Problems

It is important to listen not only to what you're told in words, but also to what you're shown by expression and gesture. Sympathetic listening is needed most when a friend, a lover or a member of your family comes to you with a problem. If you're going to be any help, you'll have to listen to the facts of the problem, but you'll also have to pick up from the tone what it is that your friend *feels* about what's happened. This often requires you to say very little in words, but a great deal in the tone of the words you do use and in your expressions and gestures.

Listen to Tape Extract 8 and look at the photographs below of Anne's face as she listens sympathetically to the problem.

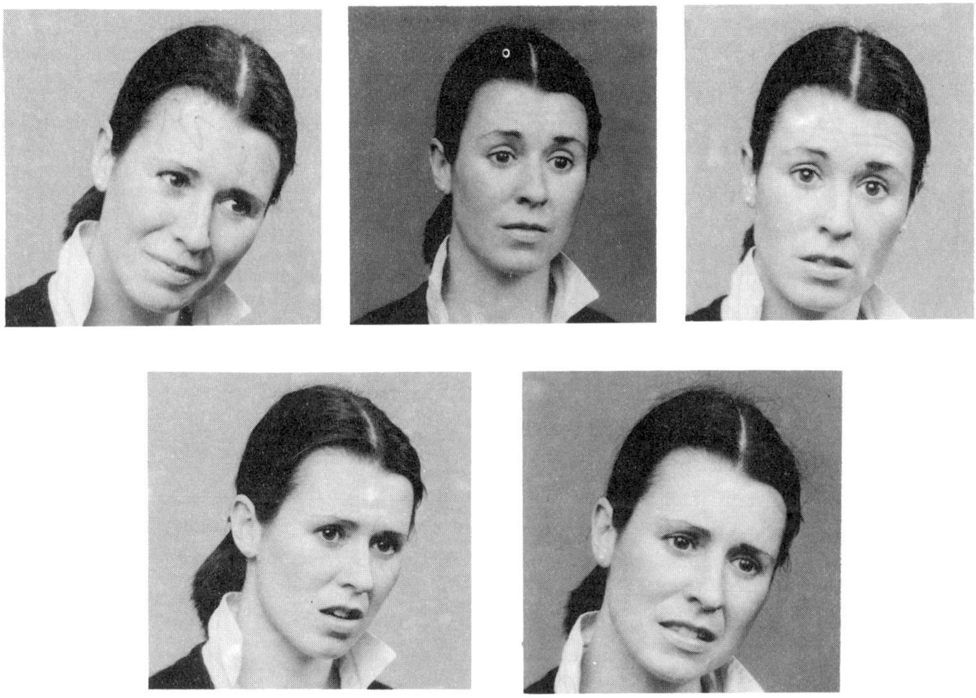

TAPE EXTRACT 8

Do you think Anne helped Declan at all? How else could she help him to sort out his problems?

3.9 Guidelines

Here are some guidelines to sum up the main things to remember about effective listening:

- *try to be interested.* You'll listen a lot better if you are.
- *focus your listening* either by using a list of *questions* as a guide, or by asking yourself 'What do I want to know?' as you listen. *Making notes* can help you concentrate.

– in some cases, it's not enough simply to get the facts. Sometimes the facts are less important than the speaker's feelings. So *listen sympathetically*.

– listening sympathetically means listening for the tone behind what someone says. If you can *identify the tone*, you can deal with it efficiently.

– don't just listen to the words someone says, *look at their face and body* for clues on tone.

– *keep an open mind*. Try hard not to allow a person's appearance or accent prejudice your attitude to what they say.

Extended Exercise – 'The Seagull Retreat'

Work in groups of six. In each group, one person is the hotel receptionist at The Seagull Retreat, a small hotel by the sea, and the others are prospective guests. (You'll find descriptions of the guests in Appendix One, on page 113.) When guests come to the hotel desk to make their reservations, the receptionist has to fill in the two forms on page 32.

Information for the receptionist

As each guest comes to your desk, find out the information you need to fill in each of your forms. You should have a copy of each form in front of you. Try to answer any of the questions they ask you, and remember to listen for their tone. Tell each guest which room you have allocated to them.

Room 1 Double with shower. Sea view. Balcony.
Room 2 Double with shower. Sea view. Balcony.
Room 3 Double with bath. View of gardens.
Room 4* Double with shower. View of gardens.
Room 5 Double with bath. Sea view.
Room 6 Double with bath. View of gardens.

* Room 4 is already reserved for the whole week for regular visitors, the Kluger family, from West Germany.

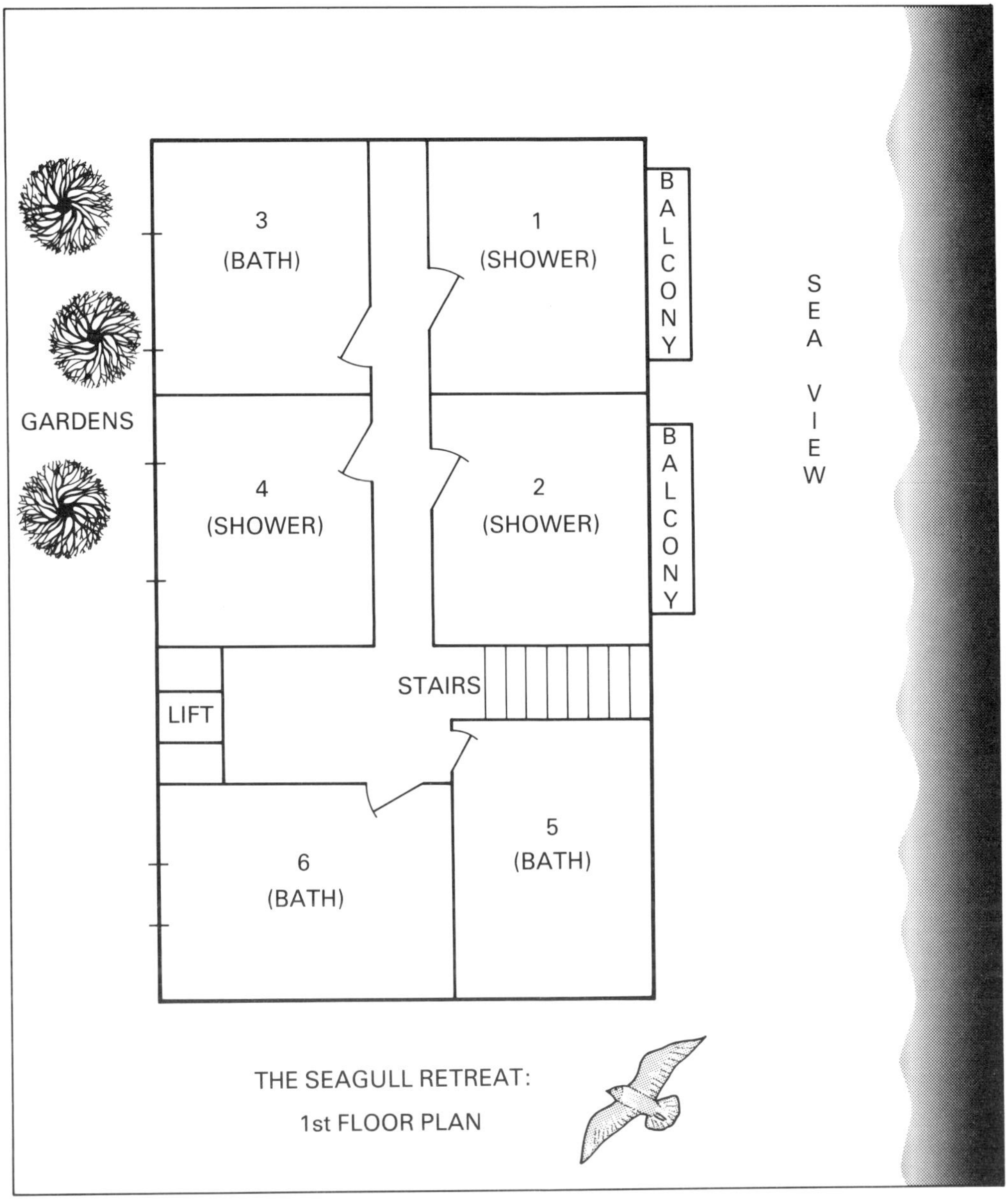

Child's Cot – Free
Single Room Supplement – £3 per night. (But no extra charge to guests wanting only bed and breakfast.)
Bed and Breakfast – £15 per night for a double room.
Half Board – £15 plus £5 per person per night.
Full Board – £15 plus £10 per person per night.

NB All guests must leave their rooms by 10.30 a.m. and can only book in after 12 noon.

FORM 1

(to be completed for each guest)

(tick appropriate column for nights stayed in hotel)

NAME:

ADDRESS: TEL:

DATE:	F/B	H/B	B & B	TIME OF DEPARTURE	SPECIAL NOTES
MON. 12th					
TUES. 13th					
WED. 14th					
THU. 15th					
FRI. 16th					
SAT. 17th					
SUN. 18th					

ROOM ALLOCATED:

FORM 2 - OVERALL ROOM PLAN

(tick appropriate column for nights stayed in hotel)

WEEK COMM. 12/9	ROOM 1 Sea / Shower	ROOM 2 Sea / Shower	ROOM 3 Garden / Bath	ROOM 4 Garden / Shower	ROOM 5 Sea / Bath	ROOM 6 Garden / Bath	TOTAL H/B	TOTAL B & B
MON.				√				
TUES.				√				
WED.				√				
THUR.				√				
FRI.				√				
SAT.				√				
SUN.				√				

4

Help and Advice

4.1 Asking for Help and Advice

Everyone needs help and advice at some time in his/her life. Nobody knows everything. But sometimes it can be difficult to ask for the help you want. It can also be difficult to give people the advice they need.

One of the most important parts of giving advice is seeing other people's points of view. What is it that they want? What difficulties are they having? The first part of this chapter is on *getting* advice and help. Once you've seen some of the things that get in the way, then it's easier to look at the ways you can *give* advice and help to others.

When you have to ask for something, you feel at a disadvantage from the start. You're admitting that another person has more knowledge or resources than you have. You feel as if you're putting yourself in their power. Perhaps that's a rather extreme way of putting it – but that's often the way it seems. Then there are the occasions when you know you need advice, but you're not sure exactly what it is you want. It's all rather vague. You need help to define what it is you need help for . . . And even when you know exactly what it is you want you have the problem of not knowing quite how to go about asking for it. Getting a loan from the bank manager, for example. Is there some special way it's done? And when you get to talk to the bank manager, you may find you don't understand what he or she says to you. The person you're talking to may think you know more than you do. For example, the expert who is always using initials to refer to something you've never heard of. And because you feel at a disadvantage anyway, you don't like to admit that you don't understand. So you're left back where you started. Getting advice and help isn't easy. But it is essential, because nobody can be an expert in everything.

4.2 Careers Counsellor

Take the occasion when you don't know exactly what you want. Listen to Tape Extract 9.

TAPE EXTRACT 9

How could David have made the interview on the tape more satisfactory? Work with a partner. Each of you in turn should take the rôle of a person going to see a careers counsellor. Use your own situations as a basis and work out an interview where you come away with more useful information than David did. Here are a few points to bear in mind:

1 Give the counsellor full information at the start of the interview. For example, your age; the course or subjects you are taking at the moment; any exams you have already got; what you might be interested in; your part-time work; any particular interests which might affect your job choice (e.g. working as a DJ in your own time; making model aeroplanes or your own clothes).

2 If you *might* be interested in staying on at college, say so, even if this is unlikely. There could be courses you don't know about which might interest you.

3 Ask about job training schemes, e.g. day release; evening classes; government training.

4 Make sure you ask for booklets, leaflets etc. which you can look at at your leisure.

5 Don't let the counsellor hurry you out before you're ready. You're as entitled to their time as anyone else. But do be polite. It doesn't help to annoy people when you want their advice.

4.3 Asking for a Bank Loan 1

The business of asking a bank manager for a loan is difficult for everyone. You may not get every loan you ask for, but there's no reason why you shouldn't ask. A bank manager is there to help you. But you can make it difficult for yourself. Listen to Tape Extract 10. What goes wrong with Mr Singh's application for a loan?

TAPE EXTRACT 10

On Tape Extract 11 there's another example of a young person, Mr Patel, asking for a loan. This time it's more successful. Why?

TAPE EXTRACT 11

Mr Patel didn't let his feeling of being at a disadvantage interfere with what he wanted. He allowed the bank manager to give him information he didn't have. He also let the bank manager ask most of the questions, although he made sure that he did ask about things he really wanted to know. In other words, he allowed the bank manager to help him. Mr Singh made that impossible by trying to be in control of things he knew nothing about.

4.4 Asking for a a Bank Loan 2

Work in pairs and prepare an interview between a bank manager and someone asking for a loan.

Information

The applicant is 18 years old and has been working for two months. He/she earns £2800 p.a. after deductions (tax, National Insurance, etc) and has £200 saved from earlier part-time work while at college. Choose one of the following reasons for wanting a loan:
a) For a car or motorbike.
b) For a holiday.
c) For moving into a flat – rent in advance and moving and furnishing expenses.

Consider i) How much you would want to borrow.
ii) How much you could afford to pay back each month.
iii) How long you would want for repayment.

Bank manager's notes for guidance on loans to young persons

1 Has the applicant got a job? Is it reasonably secure? How long has s/he been employed? How much does s/he earn?

2 Is the applicant under 18?

3 Is the monthly repayment a reasonable one in view of applicant's salary? (i.e. is it 20% or less after other deductions?)

4 What other regular expenses does applicant have, e.g. rent, payment to parent?

5 Can applicant suggest a guarantor?*

6 Any savings? Regard regular saver as a good risk.

7 Does the applicant seem a sensible and trustworthy person?

8 Give applicant clear information on repayment amounts and terms. (For repayment tables, see Appendix Two, pp. 114–117.)

9 Don't permit more than a two-year repayment period.

10 In the case of motor bike purchase insist on life insurance cover.

* A guarantor is an adult who would be prepared to pay off your debt for you if you got into difficulties, e.g. a parent, guardian or friend.

4.5 Gobbledegook

Most people find it difficult to admit that they don't understand what's said to them. If you're already feeling at a disadvantage it becomes even harder. Take the case of a student sitting in a classroom listening to a lecture on a new subject. The lecturer is confident and talks as though everyone knows a lot about the subject. Everyone else seems to be busy writing notes even though you know they've had no more preparation than you have. The temptation is to creep out at the end, say nothing and hope that no one will ask you any questions. Listen to Tape Extract 12.

TAPE EXTRACT 12

The student on the tape tried hard but didn't get much help from the lecturer. However, perhaps she gave up too soon. Listen to the tape again. What other questions would you have asked? Alternatively, how would you have explained to the lecturer that what he was saying was way over your head and perhaps also over the heads of the other students in the class?

The 'tattoo' with a fruity scent

IF YOU see someone walking down the street, covered with gaily coloured "tattoos", and smelling odd, blame 3M. The company from Minnesota is now selling Scratch 'n Sniff stickers in Britain, after creating a children's craze for them in the US.

The stickers rely on the same technology as 3M's office planner system and "Post-it" note pads. These are yellow slips of paper which can be stuck to letters, by pressure, peeled off, and re-used hundreds of times if necessary. The secret is that the glue is contained in tiny spheres made from urea formaldehyde resin, which rupture under finger pressure. The spheres are between 15 and 40 micrometres in diameter. Each time the note paper is pressed, a few more spheres rupture to release a fresh film of glue.

Scratch 'n Sniff stickers use microspheres of glue for sticking to the skin, but they also have a coating of microspheres on the upper surface. These contain perfume. Each sticker has around 4 million spheres and each scratch ruptures between 20 and 40 000 to release another sniff of scent. Tattoo wearers can scratch their stickers 200 times and still smell the result. In Britain, 3M is selling fruit flavours—banana, strawberry and orange. In the US children can buy stickers flavoured with beer, dry martini and freshly minted money. □

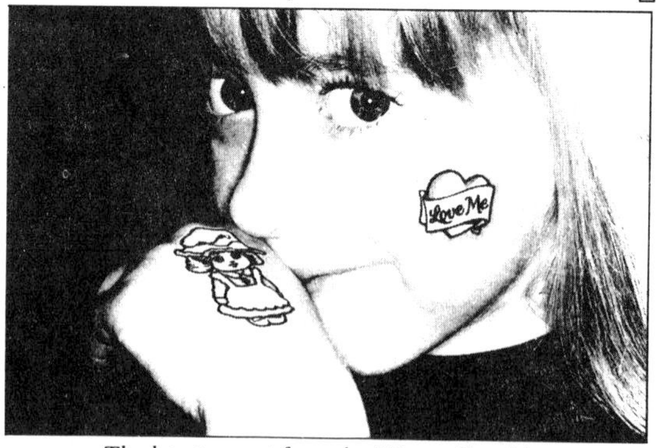

The latest export from the US: smelly stickers

4.6 Superman and the Tattoo

The two articles reprinted here from *New Scientist* give two items of technological news. Read the articles and then for each one, select someone from the group who feels reasonably confident that they can understand and answer questions on it. Then the rest of the group should ask questions until everyone is absolutely clear about what the handouts mean.

Superman flies in 3-D

SUPERMAN may soon fly in 3-D. Zoran Peristic created the special effects which enabled Superman and woman to fly so convincingly in the recent series of superperson films. Now in British patent application 2 135 470, Peristic claims new technology for producing similar special effects in 3-D.

3-D films are made with two cameras which run side by side, capturing left and right eye images. It is difficult to create special effects in 3-D, for instance photograph an actor in front of a background, such as street scene—which has previously been filmed, because the background must itself be filmed and projected in 3-D. Otherwise the actor will be in 3-D and the background will be 2-D. Peristic suggests using a camera which has two spaced mirrors at the front. One "sees" the left eye image and the other the right eye image. Another mirror, on a rotating wheel, spins facing them so that the camera film records left and right eye images alternately on separate frames of a single film. This film runs at twice normal speed, 48 frames a second instead of 24, so that it records enough images to produce separate left and right recordings. The 3-D background scene is projected as a series of alternate left and right images, in synchronism with the left and right mirror switching on the camera. So the final film images are a 3-D blend of foreground and background.

The camera operator can see a 3-D view by looking through a modified view finder. This has a spinning mirror to separate out the left and right eye images through a pair of binoculars. □

4.7 Guidelines

These guidelines sum up what we've covered so far about asking for help and advice:

- the expert is there to help you. If you feel anxious, let him or her ask the necessary questions. *Don't think that you have to control the interview.*
- *never be afraid to ask questions yourself* about something that appears obvious to your expert but isn't to you. Some people, for example, use a great many abbreviations or jargon words in their work – don't be afraid to ask for an explanation.
- *don't get angry* about being ignorant or asking for help.
- *give* as much *relevant information* about yourself and your situation as you can.
- *don't let yourself be rushed.* You're entitled to a reasonable amount of time.
- never be afraid to *go on saying that you don't understand.* Continue to ask politely for explanations and simplifications if you don't grasp the point straight away.

4.7 The Eighteenth Birthday Party

Giving help and advice can also be difficult. Before you can give really useful advice you need to find out the answers to some questions. Suppose a friend comes to you and asks for advice on what to do about his or her eighteenth birthday party. How would you go about giving this advice? Work with a partner, who should act as the person wanting advice. Using the magazine tips given opposite as a guide, ask your friend some questions so that you can find out what he or she has in mind. Then together plan the party, remembering good parties that you've given or been to in the past.
The kind of general questions you should ask are:

1 What exactly does this person want? For example, does s/he plan to have a huge party for everyone s/he knows? Is the party only for a select group of friends? Are relations and older people going to be invited?

2 What are his/her circumstances? For example, how much can s/he afford? Will s/he have to pay for it all or will parents help? Will his/her home be big enough? Do his/her parents object to the party?

3 How much does s/he already know? For example, has s/he given many parties before?

4 How much detail do I need to give? For example, should I say anything about the kind of music or food?

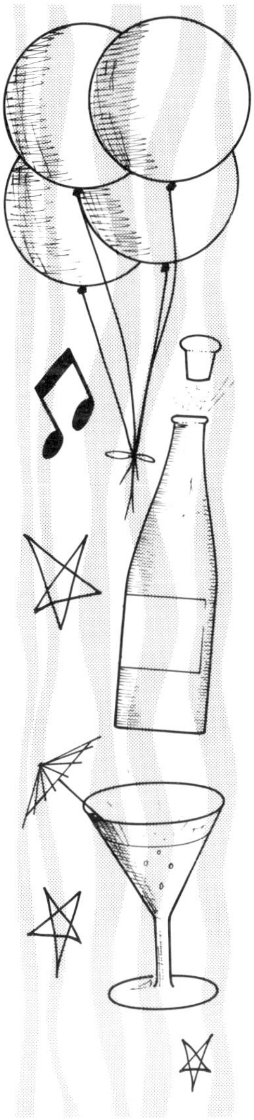

18th Birthday?

How to have a really Wild Time!

1. Place.....Home or hall?

Home

a) Is there enough room?
b) Will your parents go out?
c) Think how best to avoid damage.

Hall

a) Ring round your local pubs to see if any of them have a cheap room to rent.
b) Find out how late you can stay and if there are any restrictions.

2. Food and Drink

Food

a) Food you can eat with your fingers is best - sandwiches, chicken, lettuce etc - not so messy.
b) Keep it fairly simple - you won't want to have to work through your own birthday.

Drink

a) Make it a bottle party, but do provide a few bottles to start people off.
b) Keep a reserve for good friends at the end of the party - but don't advertise the fact.

3. Guests

a) Send out proper invitations, otherwise everyone will think any old person can come along.
b) Gatecrashers - decide what you're going to do and stick by it.

4. Music

a) Make sure it's loud enough, but don't annoy the neighbours.
b) Get someone reliable to look after the stereo.
c) Have a fairly broad choice of music so that most people can enjoy something.

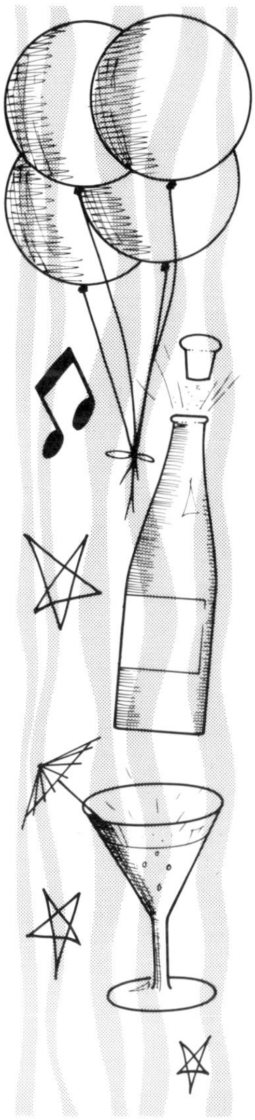

4.8 Advice on Police Powers

The last exercise was an example of how you can give advice in a casual kind of way – more of a discussion, perhaps. However, there are occasions when the advice you're asked for is not so casual, when it's important that you get it right, *and* that you get it across. On the next page you'll see printed a National Council for Civil Liberties leaflet on police questioning. You work in a young people's advisory centre and have been asked to give a short talk on police questioning. You should try to be clear and informative and at the same time keep your tone friendly and informal. However, you must be careful not to sound as if you are advising your audience how to obstruct the police in their duties. Remember that you are talking to a young audience who may have already had encounters with the police. Prepare notes for your talk and then give it to the rest of the class.

Know your Rights **NCCL Fact sheets**

Police Questioning

This factsheet explains your rights if you are questioned by the police.

Usually, when the police ask for your help, you will want to give it. But you should know your rights and know when you are legally obliged to co-operate.

The Judges Rules

Police questioning is covered by the Judges Rules. These Rules also apply to the British Transport Police. The effect of the Rules is set out in this fact sheet.

The Judges Rules do not have the force of law. If the police disobey them — and they often do —

- *The evidence obtained can still be used in court if the judge allows it.*
- *They may have committed a criminal or disciplinary offence, or you may be able to bring an action for damages.*

Arrest

The police have no power to detain you for questioning without first arresting you. In a few situations (eg if you are driving a car) you have to give your name and address. This is explained in more detail in the fact sheet on Arrest. The police also have the power to stop and search you for drugs, firearms, stolen property (some parts of the country only) and evidence relating to terrorism. The fact sheet on Search gives more details.

Right to silence

Except in those cases where you have to give your name and address only, you do NOT have to answer police questions or make any statement. But under the Prevention of Terrorism Act, it is a criminal offence not to give the police information about terrorism which might be useful to them.

The police should

- *Inform someone 'reasonably named' by you of your arrest (unless it will hinder their enquiries).*
- *Caution you as soon as they have reasonable grounds for suspecting that you have committed an offence. This means telling you that you do NOT have to say anything, but that anything you do say can be written down and used in evidence.*
- *Caution you again when you are charged or told that you may be prosecuted.*
- *Caution you again if further questions are asked on another occasion. You should not be questioned again after you are charged unless it is to clear up a misunderstanding in what you've already said, or to prevent loss or harm to someone else.*
- *Record both questions and answers in full, the time and place of questioning and who was present.*
- *Ask you to sign a record of their questioning. But it is often better to refuse to sign until you have talked to a lawyer. You should never sign unless you are satisfied that it is a completely accurate record of what took place.*
- *Make reasonable arrangements for your comfort and refreshment.*

The police should not

- *Make you answer questions before or after arrest.*
- *Make any promises or threats in order to persuade you to make a statement.*
- *If you are under 17, interview you without the presence of a parent, a legal adviser or some other independent person.*
- *If you are at school, question you there except if there's no alternative and then only with the head-teacher's permission and in his/her presence.*

Making a statement

You do not have to make a statement if you do not want to.

- *If you are suspected of an offence it is sensible to say something like: 'I do not want to say anything until I have seen my solicitor.'*
- *If you are charged with an offence and want to make your innocence clear, you should say something like: 'I didn't do that' or 'I am innocent.' You should not go into further explanations or answer questions until you have taken legal advice. If you are in any doubt, say nothing until you have had legal advice.*

If you do decide to make a statement, it is often better to write it yourself. Or else you can dictate it to a police officer. The statement should be in your own words without prompting, and should be read back to you. It is often better to refuse to sign it until you have talked to a lawyer. You should never sign until you are satisfied that it is correct and says exactly what you want to say. If you are unhappy about anything in it, don't sign.

Foreign languages

If English is not your first language, you should make a statement in your own language.

Seeing a lawyer

The police should let you contact a lawyer, although they needn't do this if it would 'hinder the investigation.' In practice, this means that people usually aren't allowed to contact a lawyer until after the police have finished questioning.

You have the right to speak to the lawyer alone, and you can insist that he is present before answering any questions. Remember that any conversation with your lawyer on the phone may be overheard.

Fingerprints

The police do not have the right to fingerprint you unless you agree. Once you have been charged with an offence, they can apply to the magistrates' court for an order allowing them to take fingerprints even without your consent. If in doubt, ask to see the order. If you are not charged or you are acquitted, fingerprints taken by order must be destroyed.

Someone aged under 14 cannot be fingerprinted at all, except with the consent of the parents or guardian.

Photographs

The police have no powers to photograph you at the police station. You can refuse to be photographed — but if they photograph you anyway, there is nothing much you can do except complain. If you are remanded in prison before your trial, the magistrate can give a warrant allowing you to be photographed.

Prevention of Terrorism Act

If you are held under this law, the police can photograph and fingerprint you without your consent, and without getting a warrant. The prints and photos will be kept after you are freed, even if you are not charged with an offence.

4.9 Looking After Yourself

Finally, there's the important area of *how* you give advice or help – namely your tone. People can be very easily hurt or embarrassed if your tone is wrong; they may think you're being patronising or rude, even if you mean well. Subjects like overweight or spotty skin are examples of very personal problems where people often need help. But you need to be extremely sensitive to the other person's feelings if you're not going to make them feel worse.

Work in small groups. Each of the groups should choose one of these topics—smoking, alcohol, keeping slim—and read the relevant information given below. Then discuss the topic fully in your group, saying how each of you feels about it. For example, if you choose smoking as your topic, you might talk about how you'd like to stop smoking but find it hard, or how much you dislike bans on smoking at home or on trains and so on. Then work out some of the ways you'd advise the rest of the class on problems to do with your topic. Finally, talk to the whole class, asking them for questions and opinions and giving the advice that you've worked out in your group.

What you can do

Stop smoking. There is no miracle method for stopping smoking. If you have tried before without success, don't worry too much: most of those who give up successfully do so on their second or third attempt.

If you are serious about giving up cigarettes, it's worth giving some thought to what is, after all, an important change in your life: becoming a non-smoker.

There are four main stages in giving up:

1. You think about your reasons for stopping.
2. You prepare to stop.
3. You do it. Just stop.
4. You stay stopped.

1. Think about stopping

Do you really want to stop? Lots of people have been surprised how easy it was to stop once they had really made up their minds.

To help you make your decision, think about what you gain by stopping.

Right away ■ You'll be free from an expensive and damaging habit. ■You'll have much more money to spend. ■ You'll smell fresher. No more bad breath, stained fingers or teeth. ■ You'll be healthier and breathe more easily - for example, when you climb stairs or run for a bus. ■ You'll be free of the worry that you may be killing yourself.

For the future ■ You'll lose your smoker's cough. ■ You'll suffer fewer colds and other infections. ■ You'll avoid the dangers that smokers have to face. ■ Your children are less likely to start smoking. ■ You'll have more money to spend.

2. Prepare to stop

Break the habit. Smoking is a habit that's closely linked to certain times and places. If you break these links, you can break the habit. The best way of doing this is to avoid the situations where you want a cigarette. If you can't avoid them, then you'll have to fight off the temptation.

Sit down and think about when and where you usually have a cigarette. For example, do you always have one after breakfast? After other meals? In breaks at work? Once you stop smoking, these times and places are going to be the danger spots, so work out now how you are going to cope with them.

It will also help if you can make new habits to break the old one of smoking. So plan some new activities to replace smoking – things to distract yourself, things to do with your hands, and different ways to cope with tension.

Some people find it helps if they cut down on cigarettes before they actually give up. It's one way of preparing for the day you stop for good. But don't look on cutting down as an alternative to giving up, and don't do it for more than a couple of weeks at the very most. The danger is that you go back to smoking as many as you did before.

Get some help. Try to get some help from your friends and family. ■ Get them to sponsor you to stop. ■ Make a bet with someone that you will stop for so long – say, three months. ■ Make an agreement to stop with someone else. ■ Talk to your family. ■ Tell them what you are going to do and why. ■ Ask them to help by being patient.

Pick a day. Decide when you are going to stop. Make it a day when you will not be under much stress. The day before, get rid of all your cigarettes, ashtrays and lighters.

3. Stop

A big day. Stopping smoking for ever seems like a big step. So just take it one day at a time. Make the first day a big day. Maybe stay in bed extra late – or get up specially early. Have an extra long bath. Have fruit juice for breakfast – the taste is fresh and the acidity will help get rid of the nicotine. Plan a treat for the end of the day as a reward for not smoking.

Change your routine. Put your planning and preparation into practice. Try hard to change your routine so you avoid the situations in which you know you'll get a strong urge to smoke. The more you change your routine, the easier it will be to stop. You won't have to avoid the danger situations for ever but just for a few weeks until you have learnt to cope better with the urge to smoke.

Do something else. If you do feel a strong urge to smoke, then the important thing is to do something else instead.

Side effects will pass. Remember that up until now you have probably taken 100 to 400 puffs of tobacco every day and your body has got used to a constant supply of nicotine. At first you may be irritable and unable to concentrate. You may get wide swings of mood, happy one minute, depressed the next. You may get stomach upsets, and even a bad cough as the cleaning action in your lungs gets started. If you do get any of these effects, don't worry. It may take some time to establish the habit of not smoking. Any side effects are all part of the process of getting better and should pass in a few weeks. If they do go on longer, then check with your doctor.

You may get no bad effects at all! Many people find they get all the benefits of stopping with very few or none of the problems.

What about my weight? You may find you put on a bit of weight when you stop smoking, but this is usually only temporary. Those extra few pounds can be lost again by being careful about what you eat. You'll find some helpful advice on page 19.

4. Stay stopped

Keep at it. After your first enthusiasm has worn off, keep at it. Don't let yourself slip back. Don't smoke any cigarettes at all.

Practise looking in the mirror and saying 'No thanks, I don't smoke'. That will help you to cope with smokers who press you to smoke.

Put aside the money you would have spent on cigarettes and watch it grow.

Give yourself lots to do. Clean the house, do some decorating, get out more. Go to places where you wouldn't think of smoking.

Do something active. Play some sport. Go for walks or for a run. Get others to join you so you can share the pleasure. If you found it easy to stop, you may think you could have the odd cigarette and stop again any time you want to. Don't kid yourself: next time might not be as easy. Also, there's part of you that wants to start smoking again and will find all sorts of excuses to smoke – 'One cigarette won't hurt', 'This wasn't a good time to stop', 'Maybe I'll wait until I find a painless cure', and so on.

Don't be taken in by these excuses. There is no magic cure. It's up to you. You just have to work at breaking the habit.

Keep reminding yourself of the benefits you've gained by stopping: you smell fresher, you breathe clean air, you have more money, and most important of all, you are much less likely to die young.

Most people who give up smoking do so without outside assistance. But if you need extra advice either before you give up or if you are tempted to go back to cigarettes, why not go to see your family doctor? Or your local health education unit might run a stop smoking clinic in your area. (To find your health education unit, look in your phone book under the name of your local health authority.)

THE TRAFFIC-LIGHT GUIDE TO STAYING SLIM

HERE is a very simple way to choose the foods that'll keep you slim and in shape and feeling great. And you don't have to count calories.

Below are listed all the main sorts of foods divided into three groups according to their calorie *concentration* – ranging from RED (high in calories) through AMBER (medium in calories) to GREEN (low in calories).

Obviously, *how much* you eat is as important as *what* you eat. But even small quantities of RED-group foods contain as many calories as quite large helpings of GREEN-group foods.

Use the three groups to discover a sensible balance which suits you.

RED – stop and think

Sugar, sweets, chocolate, cakes, pies, sweet pastries, biscuits, heavy puddings, honey, syrup, treacle, jam, marmalade, fruit tinned in syrup, cream, butter, margarine, lard, cooking oil, fat on meat, salad dressing, salad cream or mayonnaise, chips, crisps, peanuts.

AMBER – go carefully

Fatty meats (like bacon or salami), sausages, liver paté, eggs, milk, oily fish (like herring, mackerel, sardines, tuna, salmon), cheese (except cottage cheese), thick creamy soups, nuts, bread (white or wholemeal), rice, pasta (like spaghetti and macaroni), savouries. Wines, beer and cider. Aperitifs, spirits and liqueurs. Most soft drinks and mixers.

GREEN – go right ahead

Fresh fruit, salads, green and root vegetables including potatoes (not fried), whitefish, seafood, poultry, game, lean meat, kidneys, cottage cheese, yoghurt (natural), skimmed milk, bran, wholegrain cereals, clear soups. Low-calorie soft drinks, coffee and tea (without sugar), water.

REMEMBER, it is easier to stay slim than to lose weight once you have put it on. A little care choosing what you eat and enough regular exercise will go a long way to get you feeling great.

■ Don't drink when you're going to drive or use machinery.

■ Choose coffee, tea or non-alcoholic drinks instead of alcohol sometimes.

■ If you drink with people who regularly buy rounds for each other, it's easy to end up drinking more than you want. You could say you'd rather just get your own. Others in the group may prefer that too, because buying rounds can get very expensive. Alternatively, drink slowly so that your glass stays fuller longer. 'I'm OK this time,' you can say. Choose small measures like half pints rather than pints, or alternate between alcoholic and non alcoholic drinks.

Try setting yourself limits, and then keep count of your drinks.

■ Try setting yourself limits for particular occasions. Decide how much you really want to drink before you start. Then stick to that limit. You can keep count of your drinks in various ways: write them down on a card, make marks on a beermat with your thumbnail, transfer coins from one pocket to another. Don't lose count and you won't end up drinking more than you want.

■ Pace your drinking throughout the evening. If you manage to keep to your limits, give yourself a reward – a visit to the cinema, new clothes, an extra hour in bed on Sunday morning – something you'd not usually allow yourself.

■ If you feel you're likely to drink more than you really want to, create a deliberate delay. Go somewhere for five minutes. Say to yourself, 'I'm in control of my own life.' You are. Often you'll be better able to stick to your plan.

■ Remember that getting drunk doesn't make you tall, rich, strong, handsome, smart, witty, sophisticated or sexy.

WHAT'S A

SENSIBLE LIMIT?

If you want to keep well within the safe limits, these are sensible limits to keep to.

FOR MEN

Two or three pints (or their equivalent), two or three times a week.

FOR WOMEN

Two or three standard drinks, two or three times a week.

But remember. There are times when even one or two drinks can be too much – for example, if you drink before driving or operating machinery.

HOW MUCH IS

TOO MUCH?

FOR MEN

Any man of average height and average weight who drinks more than 8 standard drinks a day (for example 4 pints of beer or 8 whiskies) is drinking too much and is likely to suffer illness related to alcohol.

FOR WOMEN

Any woman of average height and average weight who drinks more than 5 standard drinks a day (for example 2½ pints of beer, or 3 glasses of wine and 2 glasses of sherry) is drinking too much and is likely to suffer illness related to alcohol.

4.10 Guidelines

Here are some guidelines on points to remember about giving people help and advice.

– *find out exactly what they want to know.*

– *find out their present circumstances*, as this may affect the advice you give them.

– *find out what information they already have.*

– *don't give too much detail*; they may not need it and it can be confusing.

– *get the right tone*. You should show that you are understanding but don't let yourself forget the advice you have to give, even if it might not be welcome.

Extended Exercise – Phone in: The Parent Problem

Your local radio station has a weekly phone-in programme which deals with a different subject each week. This week the subject is the difficulties that arise between parents and children. A presenter/DJ, two parents, and a girl and a boy, both aged about 17, will answer questions put by people who phone in for help and advice.

The panel will be made up of five people from your group. Each person not on the panel should prepare a question to phone in. The questions could be on one of the following topics or on some quite different problem which affects the way parents and young people get on. In any case, the questions should be based on something you know about, either through your own or another person's experience. The panel should attempt to give sensible and helpful advice. In order to do so, they'll have to ask further questions of the caller, who should be prepared to answer them.

Suggested topics for questions

Staying out late
Planning to leave home
Parents disapproving of your friends
Drugs and alcohol
Smoking
Being untidy
Parents quarrelling with each other
Different treatment of brother or sister
Money
College or job – parents think one, you think the other
Rudeness
Interfering with your life

The questions might go something like this:
'My father says I've got to be in by 11 o'clock on a Saturday night. I'm 18 years old, but he says as long as I'm living in his house he makes the rules. What can I do about it'?

'My daughter will never tidy up her room. It's a most dreadful mess and I can smell cigarette smoke when I go in there in the morning. How can I get her to be tidier? She even makes a mess in the living room.'

5

Using the Telephone

5.1 Making a Phone Call

Many people hate using the phone, and there are all sorts of reasons why you might hate it. One is the business of talking to a person you can't see. Is that person being friendly or unfriendly? Helpful or obstructive? There are no clues to be got from face or body movements – everything depends on what the person says and how s/he says it. We'll be dealing with the person who receives the call in the second part of the chapter. But it's just as important for you, the caller, to give the right impression on the phone: if you're phoning about a job, for example, or making an appointment, or booking a holiday, or even telling someone you'll be late. You need to sound pleasant, and to say what you have to say as briefly and clearly as you can. You've also got to remember that the telephone distorts the voice, so you must speak particularly carefully.

There are hundreds of different reasons for making a phone call. Often you will be phoning friends and family, but here are a few typical examples of business phone calls you may have had to make:

1 Arranging an appointment at the dentist, the optician or the doctor.

2 Changing an appointment you've already made. For example, a driving lesson.

3 Putting an advertisement in the paper to sell your bike.

4 Phoning in answer to an advertisement in the paper for a job you'd really like.

5 Arranging for a plumber to come and mend a burst pipe.

6 Complaining about some stereo equipment you bought which has gone wrong.

7 Sending flowers to someone who is sick.

8 Booking a holiday.

9 Enquiring about bus or train times.

10 Reserving cinema, theatre or concert tickets.

You've probably had to make several of these kinds of call in your life and managed them quite successfully. But sometimes simple phone calls can go badly wrong. For example, those that you'll hear in Tape extracts 13 and 14.

As you listen to the tape, make a list of the mistakes you think were made in the two calls:

TAPE EXTRACTS 13 and 14

In groups, discuss the mistakes made by Fred, the caller.
Instead of spoiling those two phone calls, Fred could have made some notes before he started. For example, the notes he might have made for the second call are shown at the top of the next page:

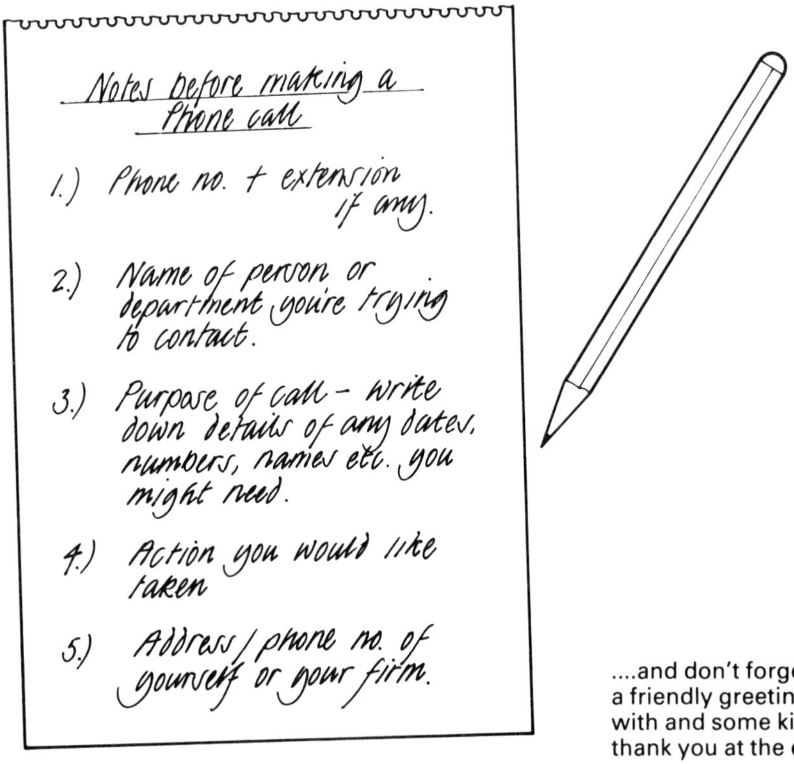

....and don't forget a friendly greeting to start with and some kind of thank you at the end.

Notes for call to Brigworth Ltd

1 657 2299
2 Ad. in yesterday's *Standard* for a toolsetter.
3 Application form.
4 Name and address.

The call would have taken about two minutes and Fred would have got what he wanted with very little bother, either for himself or the receptionist.

5.2 Making Phone Notes

Choose *one* of the examples given in 5.1. Then, using the guidelines opposite, make a set of notes for the call like the ones Fred should have used.

In pairs, and using your notes, take turns to make your call. The person receiving the call should try to be as helpful as possible.

5.3 'This is a Machine Talking'

Quite often, you'll find that you won't be greeted by a real person on the other end of the line. Instead, there'll be a faint whirring sound and a recorded voice will ask you to leave a message. As an example, take number 2 in 5.1, where you had to change the time of your driving lesson. On the tape, you'll hear the recording the driving school has left:

TAPE EXTRACT 15

Here are some notes you've made for the call:

Notes for call to driving school

1 976512
2 Change lesson from Fri. 17/9 at 10.30–important interview.
3 OK any afternoon next week after 4.30.

Although you weren't expecting an answering machine, you don't immediately hang up when you hear the message; you've got no desire to pay the cancellation fee the school requires. Instead, you record on the tape all the necessary information.

With a partner to read out the recorded message on the answering machine, practise leaving your message, using the notes above.

Answering machine message

'This is the International Driving School, Blempton-on-Sea. We're out of the office at the moment, so please leave a message. Speak after the tone and give us the date and time as well as your name and number. We'll call you back as soon as we can.'

Look at the list of notes for phone calls given below and practise leaving messages for each of them. The machine you're speaking to uses much the same message as the driving school.

1 Notes for call to doctor

a) Give name
b) Appointment with Dr Mitra. Don't want to see anyone else.
c) Any evening after 5.30.
d) Please phone to confirm 693 8495.

2 Notes for call to Shilworth Ltd

a) Give name
b) Interested in job as office junior advertised in yesterday's *Standard*.
c) Tel. 78965.

3 Notes for call to plumber

a) Burst pipe.
b) 69 Woodford Road, STELHURST-ON-SEA.
c) Give name.
d) Water coming through ceiling. Please come a.s.a.p.
e) Phone 698 579.

4 Notes for call to stereo Ltd

a) Name.
b) Stereo deck bought last Fri. at store in Blenheim High Street.
c) Faulty.
d) Can it be mended by next Fri.? Urgent.
e) Phone 72345.

5 Notes for call to Flowers Ltd

a) Name.
b) Please send one dozen red tulips.
c) To Mrs Briggs, Elizabeth Bolton Ward, Elton Hospital, Elton.
d) Message to read 'Get better soon, Love Doug.'
e) Pay by Access no. 7943 6832 7904 589.

6 Notes for call to travel company

a) Name.
b) Own address.
c) Please send brochure on Italian holidays advertised on Breakfast TV today.

7 Notes for call to theatre

a) Six tickets for 'Nightime Cabaret' night of 6 June. Must be front stalls or box.
b) Reserved in name of Bolton. To be called for at box office.
c) Barclaycard no. 4630 8952 765 8884
d) Any problems plse call own name on 567 8999.

8 Notes for call to mail order firm

a) Name.
b) Own address.
c) Want to order item 79D from June catalogue – variant C5.
d) Charge to account no. CS 5609923.
e) Account holder 2 yrs standing.

For most everyday phone calls, there's a simple way of making your call more effective and less nerve-racking:

Be prepared. Write a few brief notes to help you keep to the point and to remind you of what you have to say.

5.4 Will That be All Right, Mum?

If you listened to Fred's two terrible phone calls in Tape Extracts 13 and 14 you'll remember that he made several different kinds of mistakes, and some of them would not have been helped by a set of notes. Those were the mistakes he made by being rude or abrupt or over-familiar. In other words he used the wrong tone.

At the beginning of the chapter we discussed the importance of using appropriate words and an appropriate tone. The *way* you talk to someone on the phone can

make the difference between good-natured agreement and a quarrel.

On Tape Extract 16 you can hear two brief telephone conversations. They use identical words, but very different tones. One resulted in disaster, the other did not.

TAPE EXTRACT 16

The tape extract gave a rather extreme example of the way different tones of voice can lead to totally different outcomes.

5.5 Phone Tactics

The next tape extracts show two other examples of how phone calls can go wrong.

TAPE EXTRACT 17 & 18

In groups, discuss what went wrong in those two phone calls and think how both sides could have handled what happened more tactfully.

5.6 Making Difficult Phone Calls

Choose one of the following situations. With a partner, act out the telephone conversation so that the outcome is as successful as you can make it:

1 You're phoning home to say that you're going to be back later than you promised. There was an incident last week when you arrived back at 1 a.m. when you should have been there at 11.30 p.m.

2 You're phoning a shop to complain about a pair of shoes you bought last week. The heel has come off. The shop says they have no responsibility for a fault in the shoes and you must have caused it to happen through bad treatment.

3 You're phoning a friend to break a date with him or her. You don't want there to be any bad feelings about it,so you try to be as gentle as possible.

4 You're phoning a shop where you bought a new record player. The turntable is spinning slowly and your favourite album sounds like a foghorn on a bad day. The shop says you must be mistaken and that they've never had any trouble with that model before.

5 You're phoning your uncle to say that you've crashed his car. He is very annoyed.

5.7 Guidelines

These guidelines sum up what we've covered so far about making phone-calls:

- before you use the phone, *think about the purpose* of your call.
- then *prepare some brief notes* to help you. Keep paper and pencil nearby.
- when *speaking to an answering machine,* keep calm, and give your message slowly and clearly. Don't forget to leave your name and phone number.
- think about how the way you talk will affect the person you're speaking to. *Get the right tone.*

And here are a few extra points just for good measure.

- make sure you're *talking to the right person* before starting the main business of your call.
- make a note of the *name and extension number:* you might need to call the person back.
- remember that *phone calls cost money.* It's cheapest to phone after 6 p.m. (especially long distance); and calls are most expensive between 8 a.m. and 1 p.m. on weekdays.

5.8 Answering the Phone

When you're on the other end of a call, it's more difficult to prepare for what might turn up. But there are some ways to make things easier for yourself and your caller.

To start with, there's the way you answer the phone. Listen to the tape and make a note of the greetings you prefer.

TAPE EXTRACT 19

If you think about the ones you preferred, you'll probably find that it wasn't just chance that made you pick them.

The person answering the phone spoke clearly so that you could hear properly.

S/he gave the name of the company so you knew you'd got through to the right place.

S/he sounded friendly and welcoming – but not too casual.

5.9 The Bigglesworth Weekly Courier

In many jobs there are specific things which you have to find out from the caller. For example, if you worked in the classified ads section of a local newspaper like the *Bigglesworth Weekly Courier*, you would have to find out from callers exact details of the advertisements they wanted to place. You'd have a set of guidelines to help you and a form to fill in for each caller.

Work in pairs, with one person acting as caller, and the other as receiver. The caller wishes to advertise an item (e.g. bike, skating boots, guitar) for sale; the receiver is the ads telephone salesperson who has to find out all the details.

BIGGLESWORTH WEEKLY COURIER

CLASSIFIED ADS. GUIDELINES

1. Which section should the ad. be in?
2. Rates: 10p per word (Min. 10 words).
   50p Box Number.
   £3.50 extra for Display ad.
3. Publication day - FRIDAY
   All ads. must be placed by 5 p.m. on the TUESDAY before. After that, they go in following week's issue.
4. Is the caller paying by credit card?
   If so, is it ACCESS or BARCLAYCARD - others not taken.
   What's the card number?
   Name and address of cardholder.
   Date of expiry.
5. If normal invoice required:
   a) Get name and address.
   b) Inform customer that if the invoice is paid within 7 days of the date on the invoice, there is a reduction of 10%.
6. Credit card customers pay the full amount.
7. Always read back the message and check customer's name and address.

Information for the caller

1 You want to place an ad. in this week's paper if possible. Today is Wednesday 18/9.

2 The ad. should go in the 'Articles For Sale' column, and you're not interested in a display ad.

3 You have an Access card, but you won't use it if it's going to cost more to do so. The number is: 5224 0062 3795 0349, and it expires at the end of the year.

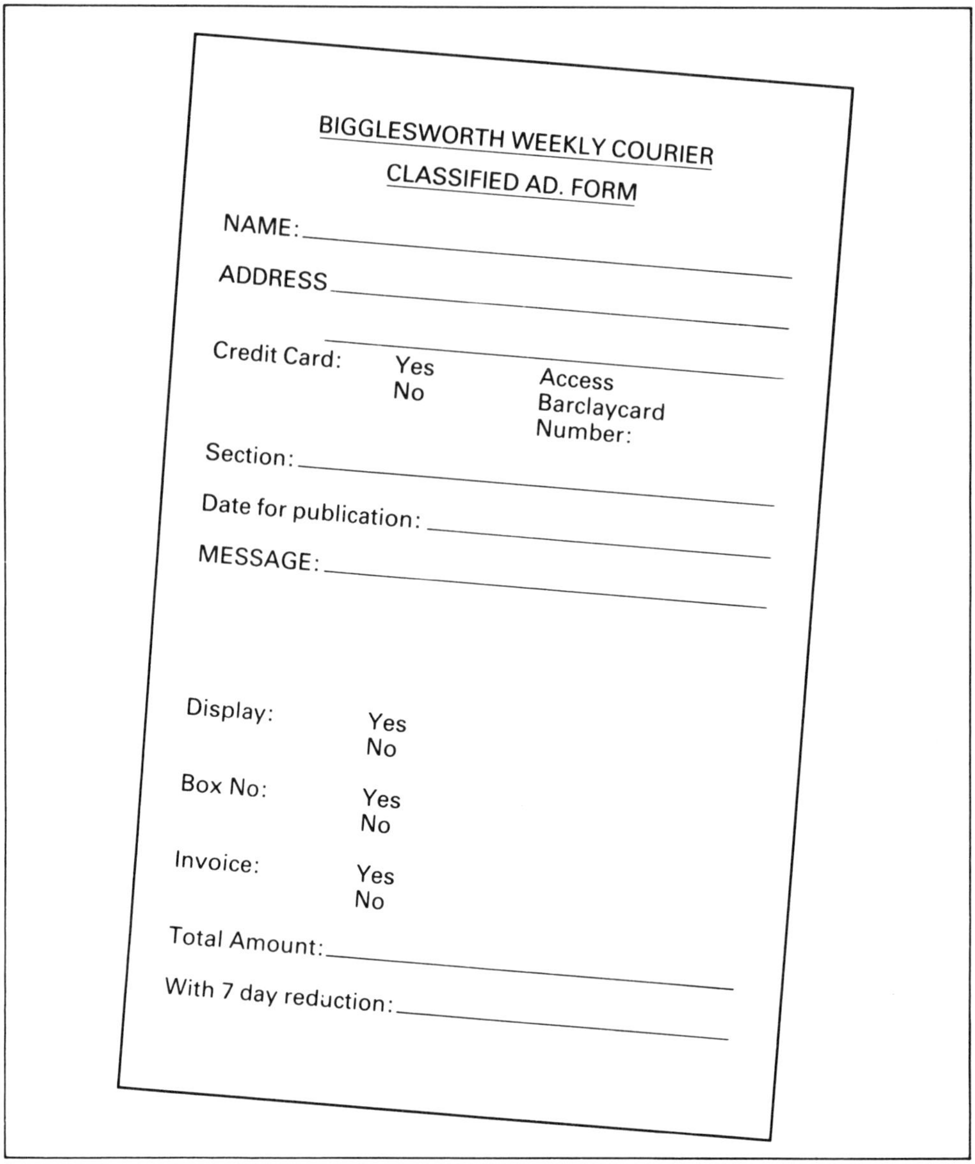

BIGGLESWORTH WEEKLY COURIER

CLASSIFIED AD. FORM

NAME: ____________________

ADDRESS ____________________

Credit Card: Yes / No — Access / Barclaycard / Number:

Section: ____________________

Date for publication: ____________________

MESSAGE: ____________________

Display: Yes / No

Box No: Yes / No

Invoice: Yes / No

Total Amount: ____________________

With 7 day reduction: ____________________

Now, close this book and write out a short ad. of between ten and twenty words for the newspaper. Remember to mention the price of the article you want to sell.

Information for the 'Courier' clerk

Your guidelines, and the form you have to fill in are printed here. First, copy the form onto a spare sheet of paper. Then, using the guidelines, ask questions to find out from the caller the information required for the form. A friendly and welcoming tone will be a help to the advertiser and create a good impression of the paper.

Using the guidelines and the information given above, make the phone call.

5.10 Barsetshire Technical College

The last exercise was a fairly straightforward process of getting specific information. But there are times when you have to deal with more difficult customers and more difficult messages. For example, there's the Confused Caller. . . .

Chris works in the student administration section of a college. He has a message pad which looks like this:

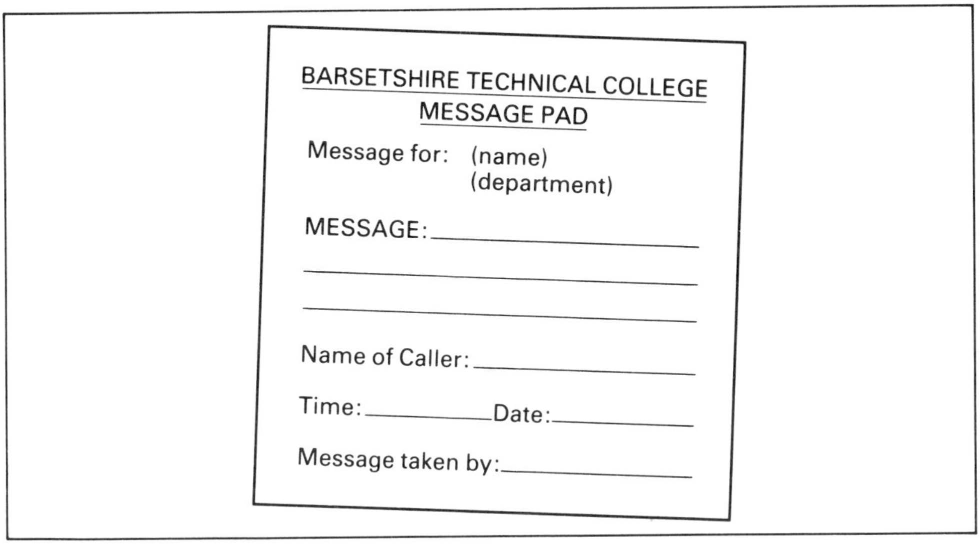
BARSETSHIRE TECHNICAL COLLEGE
MESSAGE PAD

Message for: (name)
(department)

MESSAGE: ______

Name of Caller: ______

Time: ______ Date: ______

Message taken by: ______

Chris has to fill in all the details on the message pad, even if it's a very confusing call.

If you listen to Tape Extract 20, you'll hear how one caller made life difficult for Chris.

TAPE EXTRACT 20

There *are* ways of getting some sense even out of people like Jim. You can interrupt them and ask some polite questions. Listen to the tape extract again, then:

a) Complete a copy of the message pad with as much information as you can.
b) List some extra questions you would need to put to Jim to complete the message properly.

5.11 More Difficult Calls

There are other difficult callers. For example, there's the angry caller, the shy caller and the caller you can't hear properly. Listen to the tape and think about how you would deal with each of them. First, the angry caller:

TAPE EXTRACT 21

How would you deal with Mr Smith? In groups, make a list of the things you might say to calm him down and get some proper information.

Next, there's the shy caller.

TAPE EXTRACT 22

How would you help Mrs Green? As before, discuss what you might say to get the information you need to deal with her problem and reassure her.
And then there's the indistinct caller:

TAPE EXTRACT 23

Is the situation on Tape Extract 23 hopeless? Or are there ways you could deal with that problem?

5.12 Guidelines

These guidelines sum up what we've covered so far about receiving phone-calls:

- when answering the phone, make a good impression: speak *clearly*: give the name of your company or your phone number; be *friendly* and welcoming.
- keep memo/message pad/order form next to the phone to help you to *ask the necessary questions.*
- when dealing with difficult callers: *keep calm, stay polite;* try to put yourself in their position.
- always obtain *name* and *phone number/address*, reading back to check accuracy.
- when you have made notes for a call, *pass on* any relevant *information immediately.*
- reassure your caller that you are still listening: *comment briefly* during the conversation.
- *know when to end a call*: don't let it go on too long.

Extended Exercise – Round-Britain Tour

You are helping to arrange a round-Britain tour by the rock group you work for. Using the information given below, practise and then tape the following phone calls. Work with a partner so that one of you acts as caller in (a) and the other as receiver. Then in (b) you should reverse the roles. Each of you should act as caller in (c). In all cases, the caller should make notes in preparation for the call.

1: Parkside Hall, Stockton

Caller:
You have to phone your friend, who runs the Parkside Hall, Stockton (tel. 0642 321433), to ask if s/he can book the band into his/her hall for the nights of Friday 7th and Saturday 8th August. S/he'll have to arrange pre-publicity, ticket sales and refreshments. You'll bring all the lighting and sound equipment you need.

Receiver:
You run the Parkside Hall, Princes Street, Stockton. You haven't heard from your friend for about a year, so you're quite surprised to hear from him/her. You're a bit worried about how reliable s/he is, and anyway, you've already got a provisional booking for Friday 7th and Saturday 8th August. However, you haven't yet received any money from the other people, and you like the thought of the profits you think you'll make from the sales of drink and refreshments. So you tell your friend that if s/he can get you a cheque for the deposit of £150 before the other people pay up, you'll let the band have the booking.

2: Gainsborough Hotel, Stockton

Caller:
A few days later, when you've got the hall booking sorted out, you have to phone the Gainsborough Hotel, Stockton (tel. 0642 69168). You want to book rooms for the the five members of the band, two roadies and yourself for the two nights you're going to be in Stockton. You'll need to tell the hotel that you'll be keeping late hours and that there could be reporters etc. milling around. You'd also like to book a room suitable for a press conference on Friday evening.

Receiver:
You are the assistant manager of the Gainsborough Hotel. You know that your boss has had some bad experiences with rock bands on previous occasions and is unlikely to be keen on the booking. However, if s/he accepts it, the booking is likely to bring in quite a lot of money and publicity for the hotel. You aren't able to make the final decision, but you want to get some kind of reassurance from the tour organisers that there'll be no bad behaviour, use of drugs, police appearances or upset of other guests. You arange to phone back when you've spoken to the manager. Write notes for a brief talk for him.

3: Vanhire Ltd

Caller:
You have to phone your local branch of Vanhire Ltd (tel. 752603). They are going to provide the two five-ton vans you're going to use to carry equipment for the tour. You spoke to them three days ago about your plans and you're now phoning to confirm your hire of the vans from the evening of August 1st to the morning of September 30th. The price you agreed was £60 per van per day, but you need to find out whether you have to pay the full daily rate for the first and last days of the hire. Each van is to be self-drive, so you want to double-check that the driver doesn't need an HGV licence. Insurance is to be arranged by Vanhire. When you call, you are greeted by an answering machine. Leave a message, giving the appropriate details.

Message on Vanhire Ltd answering machine

'This is Vanhire. We are sorry the office is closed at the moment. If you leave a message including your name and telephone number, we will contact you when we re-open. Beeeep. . . .'

6

Reporting

6.1 Making Reports

Reporting often seems to be a very artificial skill. After all, in real life how often do you have to stand up and make a formal report to anybody? But what you do often have to do is to tell people about what you've been doing. For example, at work, your boss might ask you what happened that morning. At home, your mother might ask what you did that day. A friend could phone and say she missed last night's episode of a TV serial – what happened? On a more formal level, you might find yourself having to tell the police about an accident you witnessed, or reporting on a week's work to your course organiser. In each case you've got quite a complicated process to go through: someone asks you a simple question and to answer properly you have to consider all the following points:

- Where do I start? Should I begin at the beginning or concentrate on a memorable event and move on from there?
- What should I include and what should I leave out?
- How much detail do I need?
- How do I make this interesting?
- What kind of audience have I got? What do they want to know?

Of course, we don't think about all these things before we talk to somebody — these kinds of decisions tend to come automatically. But it is a good idea to practise making the decisions more consciously.

6.2 Cartoon Stories

Below and on page 62, you'll see two cartoon stories. They're quite simple stories, but the idea is to make them even simpler. Choose one of the cartoon strips and sum up what has happened in one or two *brief* sentences. Tell this to the rest of the group.

1
2
3
4
5
6
7
8

6.3 A Morning at Planetts

You may have found the last exercise easy if you're good at getting straight to the point of something. But sometimes it's more difficult to arrange a whole lot of events so that they make sense to someone else. Real life is more difficult to deal with than a story – it refuses to fall into a neat order. Below, you'll see a page torn from a scribble pad and on Tape Extract 24 you'll hear some of the things that happened during a morning at a car servicing department. Using the tape and the notes made on the scribble pad, work out what you'd say in answer to your boss's question 'What happened this morning?' Bear in mind that this is the first time you've been left in charge of the office and your boss is understandably a bit anxious. Either work with a partner or tape your report, or both.

TAPE EXTRACT 24

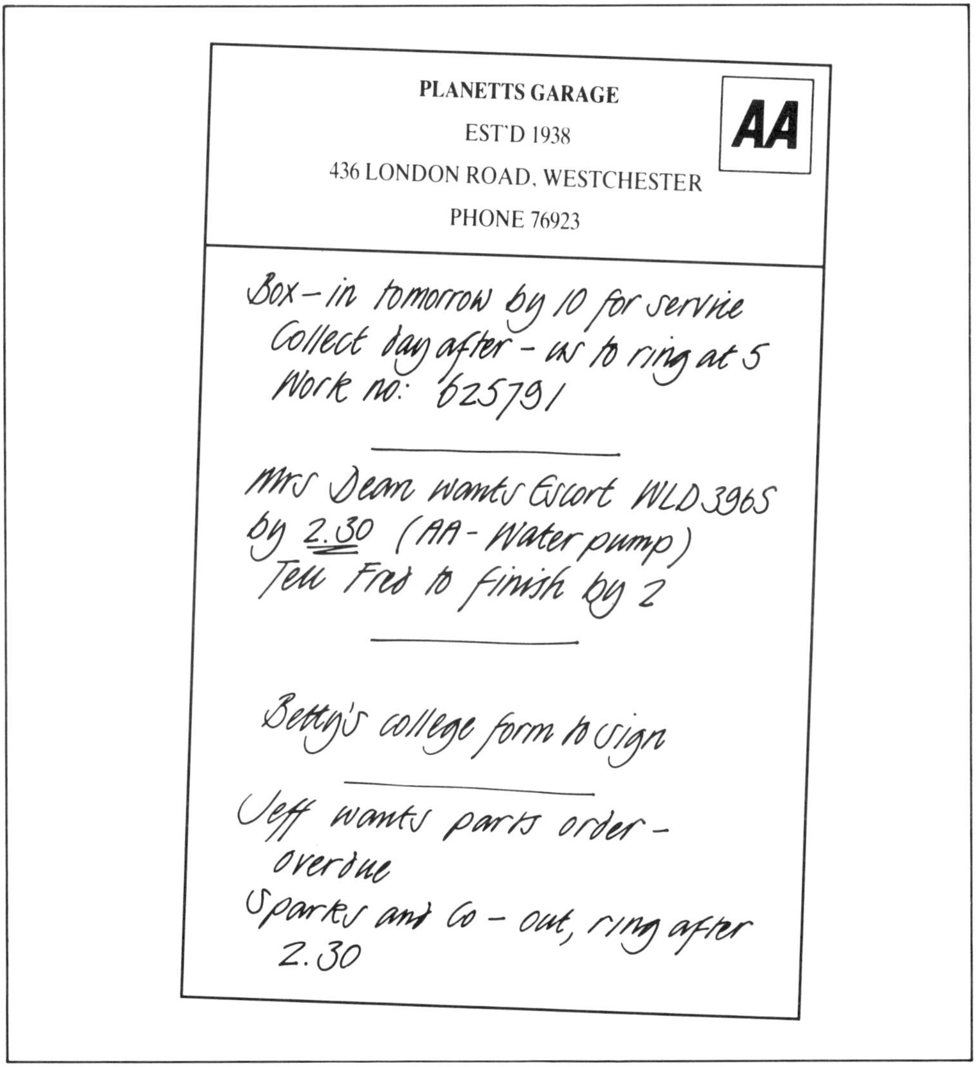

PLANETTS GARAGE
EST'D 1938
436 LONDON ROAD, WESTCHESTER
PHONE 76923

AA

Box – in tomorrow by 10 for service
Collect day after – us to ring at 5
Work no: 625791

Mrs Dean wants Escort WLD 396S
by 2.30 (AA - Water pump)
Tell Fred to finish by 2

Betty's college form to sign

Jeff wants parts order –
overdue
Sparks and Co – out, ring after
2.30

6.4 Round the College

Selecting what information you should include is also important. Too much information can be as bad as too little, because vital facts can get lost among trivial details. Working either in small groups or in pairs, make an investigation of student facilities in your college. For example, you should look at some or all of the following, each group choosing two or more items to examine.

Car park
Library
Canteen/snack bar
Noticeboards/TV screens
Sports facilities
Music and drama facilities
Medical arrangements
Students' Union
Careers advice
College newspaper
Common room
Vending machines

Your investigation could be by observation, asking staff and students, consulting a prospectus, using a questionnaire to find out opinions and so on. When you've collected your information, you should prepare a report, selecting the most important findings, and concentrating on these points:

- Describing the details of what is provided (e.g. what the union does, who runs it, how it's financed etc.).
- Giving your opinion and the opinion of other people you've talked to.
- Suggesting some recommendations for improvements.

6.5 The Mugging

When you tell somebody about an incident, you talk in a different way to different people. You may tell them the same things, but you don't speak in the same way. Listen to Tape Extract 25. Who do you think the man is speaking to each time?

TAPE EXTRACT 25

Listen to the tape again and then discuss the following points:

- the different tone used in each – e.g. the words he chose and the way he spoke.
- the information the man chose to leave out or include.

6.6 Gilbert's Fashions

Listen to Tape Extract 26. This is a report to a course organiser on a trainee's week at work. Do you think it's a good report?

TAPE EXTRACT 26

What did you like about the report? If the same girl had been telling her friend about what happened during the week at work, how would it have been different?

6.7 My Week

Work with a partner and jot down the kind of things you each did last week. Separate what you did into two parts: first at work or college; second at home and socially. Once you've got a reasonable list of activities on both sides, practise talking about what you did at home. You'll have to imagine that this is the first time your partner has heard any of what you have to say. Next, your partner should pretend that he or she is your course organiser. You should then tell him or her what happened during your week at work or college. Helpful questions are a good idea if you get stuck.

6.8 Witness in Court

There are some occasions when a formal report is required. For example, if you have to stand up in court or in front of a committee to give evidence. Here you've got to be careful and accurate, and it helps to use notes to organise what you're going to say. If you're a witness in a court case, particularly if you were directly involved, it's even harder. You may have been suffering from shock and been thoroughly frightened. On Tape Extract 27 there's a rather jumbled account of an accident, recorded soon after the event. Listen to it, and try taking notes of the main points as you go along. It'll probably help if you hear it twice. Then prepare a report which would be suitable for a court. Don't write it out, though. Read-out statements can sound very false and with an oral report it's always better just to speak from notes – it sounds more natural.

TAPE EXTRACT 27

6.9 Guidelines

Finally, here are some guidelines to sum up the main things to remember about making an oral report:

- decide where you're going to *start,* with the main event or at the beginning.
- what information are you going to *select?* What can you leave out?
- how are you going to *order* what you have to say?
- consider your *audience.* What do they want to know? What *tone* should you use?
- if you're making a formal report, use *notes* to help you, but don't write out a statement unless you've been asked to do so.
- distinguish carefully between the *facts* of what happened and your opinions about it. Reports are usually needed as a record of *events.*

Extended Exercise – Holiday 2000

A group of young people have decided to go away for a holiday. They're going to be spending quite a lot of money between them and they want to get the best possible value. So they've asked various friends to come and talk to them about holidays they've really enjoyed. When they've heard what everyone has to say they're going to decide:

a) What *kind* of holiday they want. e.g. sun, snow, sightseeing, countryside.
b) *Where* they want to go.

You should each prepare a short talk to give to them. Use the guidelines opposite to help you, and remember that you'll be speaking to people of your own age. You should aim to make your talk last for about four to five minutes and be prepared to answer questions at the end.

Guidelines

1 Give an honest account – point out the good and bad aspects of the place.

2 Make sure that you mention:

- where you went – the name of the place and the country.
- what the weather was like.
- where you stayed – was it a hotel, boarding house, tent? Was it clean, dirty, comfortable?
- what the other people were like.
- what you could do in the daytime – e.g. shopping, beaches, sports, sightseeing or trips.
- what you could do in the evenings – e.g. restaurants, dancing, barbecues etc.
- what the food and drink were like.
- how you got there – plane, car, train etc.
- how much it cost.

3 Use stories of some of the things that happened on your holiday. What funny, strange or awful things happened to you? What were the real high spots?

4 Bring in souvenirs, postcards, maps etc. so that you have something to show people. It's a real help, for instance, if you can point to the place on a globe or map so that people have an idea where it is.

5 Say why you think it would be a good or bad holiday for the group to take.

If you can't think of a suitable holiday that you've had, get a travel brochure and pick one of the holidays that you think the group would enjoy.

When you give your talk to the rest of the class, they should ask you relevant questions. When everybody has finished, the class could discuss the various suggestions and vote on the holiday they would most like to take.

7

Making an Impression

7.1 Selling the Benefits

We all think about the impression we're making on other people. 'Do you think s/he liked me?' 'Did I sound over-confident?' 'Whatever I do it comes out wrong,' and so on. Actually, the other person is probably also worrying about the impression s/he is making. It's more effective to turn the questions round. Instead of 'What should *I* do/say/look like?' ask 'What do *they* want?' And that means considering the *benefits* of whatever it is you're selling – whether it's yourself or your car. 'What can it do for you?' is a classic advertiser's question. For example, if you're selling a millionaire his fifth large car, you don't necessarily need to point out its economic petrol consumption (though you may have hit on a cost-conscious millionaire, in which case it's your job to find that out). You might point out the benefits this car possesses which his other cars don't have. Built-in compact disc system? Gold-plated steering wheel? Special ejector seat in case of trouble?

Look at the list of customers and the list of goods and services offered opposite. Work with a partner and for each customer find one or two items from the Goods and Services list. Point out the benefits to your customer, who would quite like to have the item but raises objections as you go along. You should always try to turn an objection to your advantage. For example, if the customer protests that a pair of shoes aren't leather, you have then got the opportunity to point out that man-made shoes keep out the wet and are longer lasting.

Customers

1 A young woman in her first job as a secretary. She's planning to leave home for the first time.

2 A middle-aged man with a family. He owns his own house and is a keen DIY enthusiast.

3 An 18 year old who is planning a party for fifty friends.

4 A woman out shopping with her three children, all under 5.

5 A man in a smart suit who has left his fast sports car just outside the shop in an illegal parking place.

Goods and services

1 A brightly coloured angled clip-on lamp. It can be attached to any desk, shelf or table.

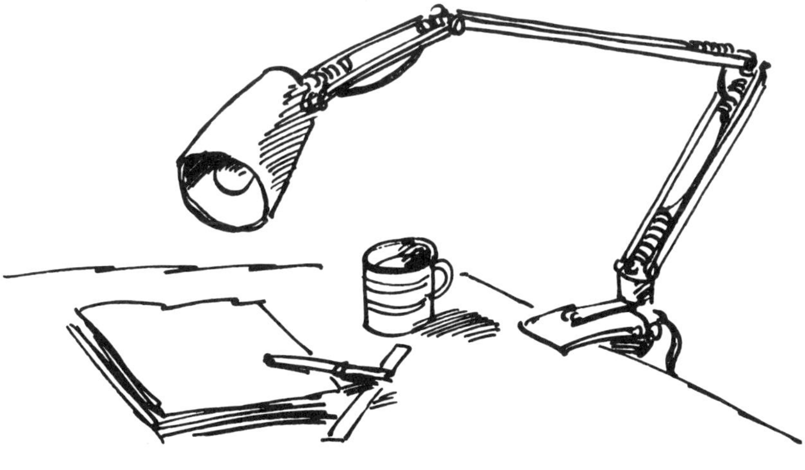

2 A set of five non-stick saucepans in electric blue. They are on special offer for a limited period only.

3 A film processing service which guarantees return within three days along with a free film. Special poster offer from your favourite negatives – half price for this month only.

4 Good quality wine and beer by the case. Delivered direct to customer's own home.

5 'Ciao Bambino' scent in gold wrapping. Special offer of an extra mini bottle with every large spray purchased.

6 A new design microwave oven which cooks whole meals in twenty minutes. A free cookery book of exotic recipes. Specially recommended for vegetables and fish. Good for making party food.

7.2 ALF – The Ford Cortina

So you point out how your product or service can benefit the customer. To do that, you've got to put things in a positive way, even when they don't seem to have much to recommend them. Before you listen to Tape Extract 28 read this description of what the salesman is selling:
Car. Ford Cortina. Resprayed gold and blue by previous owner – own work. Eight years old. Three previous owners. 80 000 miles on the clock. Bodywork rusty round boot. Brakes recently relined. Engine in reasonable condition for age but might need new clutch soon. Passed MOT 6 months ago. Taxed for 3 months. Registration number ALF 695.

TAPE EXTRACT 28

What did the salesman say to make an ordinary old car sell to his customer?

7.3 Positive Selling Points

Divide into groups. Then each of you should choose one or more of the items on the List of Objects to be sold and sell it to the rest of your group.

If you like, you could try selling something you own to the others instead. For example, a set of magazines or records; an old desk or bag; maybe some old clothes. The idea is to put across the positive points of what you're selling, while not lying or misleading your audience. Make up any necessary details, though these should be as realistic as possible. Fix any price you think you can get for the object.
As a guide, take the description of the flat given below:

FACT	POSITIVE SELLING POINTS
Small 2 bedroom flat on 7th floor of a tower block right next a station	Compact and manageable flat with 2 double bedrooms. Wonderful views and ideally placed for transport.

List of objects to be sold

1 A 15 year old car.
2 An old door from the back of your garden shed.
3 Twenty of last year's hit singles.
4 A pair of flared trousers.
5 Three pairs of old shoes.
6 An old record player your father used to have when he was young.
7 Twelve handkerchiefs with embroidered flowers in the corner.
8 A set of spanners with two missing.
9 A box of miscellaneous electrical equipment.
10 Your great uncle's hats.

You should be able to feel when you've made your sale that your customers are pleased with what they've got – and that they remain pleased with it. It's no good if they get home only to find that what you've said is untrue. Your job is simply to point out the positive side of what you're selling.

7.4 Helping the Customer

Before you get to the point of explaining benefits and putting things positively, you've got to weigh up the kind of customer you've got. What does s/he *need*? What does s/he *want*? For example, take someone going to buy a radio. He or she *needs* a small radio to use in the bedroom. He or she may *want* something in bright shiny steel with lots of winking lights. And you might have a very nice clock radio on special offer. The two sides could well do business. However, if the person who wants to buy the radio is rather shy and hates to be pushed into things, a very persuasive line would be a mistake. Something more gentle is required. For example, 'We've got quite a wide selection of smaller radios over in this section, sir/madam – if you'd just like to have a look. Just ask me if there's anything you want to know.' And the chances are that you're halfway there. How do you think the salesman or woman should continue the sale? Have you had any experiences of good or bad salesmanship? What do you think went right or wrong on these occasions?

On the question of wants and needs, it's worth remembering that sometimes what a customer wants is directly opposite from what s/he needs. For example, s/he might *need* a living room table, but s/he might *want* a bar made out of upholstered leather. It's your job as salesman or woman to resolve this conflict one way or another – either that or provide a compromise.

So there are three things you have to decide before you have a chance to make a good sale:

- what *kind of customer* have you got, and how can you tell?
- what does the customer *need*?
- what does the customer *want*?

Work with a partner and pick one or more of the following situations. One of you should act as the salesman or woman, the other as the customer:

1 *Shoe shop.* Customer comes in, hardly bothers to look round at the display. Sits down and waits for assistance. S/he needs a pair of brown shoes and wants something extremely plain and practical looking. Favours rubber soles.

2 *Electrical shop.* Customer enters, looks vaguely round at the various goods on display. Rather confused and anxious expression. S/he needs a wall lamp for a bedroom. Wants a fancy free-standing lamp with a green shade.

3 *Perfume counter.* Customer comes right up to the assistant and starts talking about the present s/he wants to buy for a particular person.

7.5 'I've Chosen This Because . . . '

Sometimes in everyday life you may find that you want to tell someone how good a particular record, band or magazine is. It's a much less specific thing to do than selling a washing machine, so possibly more difficult. You're dealing with something that is really a matter of opinion – although most of us like our friends to share in the things we enjoy. For example, how would you persuade friend to look at a particular TV programme? Say something like 'X is really good. You should watch it.'? You might add the fact that the programme is funny or exciting or has a very attractive central character, or you could explain what happened in last week's episode.

Either: 1) Choose a particular kind or piece of music you like. Put some examples on a tape and then explain to the rest of the class or group what it is you like about it, giving some examples as you go along.

Or: 2) Choose a book or magazine that you enjoy reading. Pass a copy round so that people can have a look at it and read out some short selected extracts.

Remember that in this kind of situation the most effective persuasion is your own enthusiasm.

7.6 Radio Commercial

An advertiser who wants to sell a product or service on the radio usually has to do it in thirty seconds or less. And those thirty seconds have to include the positive benefits of the product, the right atmosphere (good-humoured, romantic, powerful etc), and a means of persuading the listener to take action – immediately if possible. Commercial radio stations usually cover a fairly limited local area so they're a good place to advertise local shops, entertainments and services.

In groups of three or four, discuss good and bad radio ads you've heard and then think up some ideas for either one thirty-second or two fifteen-second ads for one of the following:

1 A charity disco to be held at a local hotel.

2 Your college rag week.

3 A new record shop which also sells musical instruments.

4 A club for 16—23 year olds opening in an old railway station.

5 A travel bureau specialising in cheap package holidays for young people.

6 A meeting-place/advice centre for young people who need help.

7 A sports centre offering facilities for all age groups.

Prepare a rough script to use when you record your ad. This should be in two columns: one for the words which will be spoken and the other for the background music, sound effects, jingles etc.

Hints on preparing a radio commercial

- Invent a slogan or jingle to help listeners remember the event or product you're advertising.
- Use rhyme, invented words or *alliteration* (several words all beginning with the same letter – e.g. 'Snappy Sisters Sell Super Socks').
- Pick out a *few* special features which you think are going to be attractive.
- Make sure you include (and repeat) essential information like date, place and time.
- Create the right atmosphere in your ad. You can do this by using humour or choosing background music to indicate a mood or including special effects – e.g. party noise etc.
- Address listeners directly as 'you'.

7.7 Dealing with Awkward Situations

It's hard to practise making the right impression in difficult circumstances, because there are so many different and unexpected occasions, but there are a few general rules you can follow. Perhaps the most important one is this:

Don't just react to what the other person *says* or to the tone they are using; instead, try to imagine what they are feeling.

Listen to Tape Extract 29. How could Janni have coped better with the news he had to give his grandmother?

TAPE EXTRACT 29

Some suggestions on how to deal with difficult situations

- Prepare people gently for bad news.
- Give them time to respond.
- Don't give feeble or dishonest excuses.
- Offer to make amends.
- Don't react immediately if they are angry – give yourself time to respond.
- Think of how they must be feeling.

Choose one of the following situations. With a partner work out how you could best cope in the circumstances.

1 You've lost your friend's dog when you were taking it for a walk in the park.

2 You've got to tell your friend's mother that s/he was injured when riding on the back of your motorbike.

3 Your employer has asked you to come to the office. S/he says that you are spending too much time talking to other employees and not doing enough work.

4 You're late for work. Your supervisor specially asked everyone to be in on time for stock-taking. You don't really have a good excuse, you just woke up late.

5 You lost your temper with your boy or girl friend last night and said some hurtful things. You want to apologise, although s/he is very angry.

6 You've got to tell a friend that you can't go on the holiday you have planned together. You've got a good reason, but you know that it's going to upset all his/her arrangements.

7.8 Interviews – On the Positive Side

In any interview the person being interviewed is trying to make a favourable impression, but this can often go wrong because the interviewee is nervous and doesn't make the best of him/herself. However, when you have to go for an interview there are ways to avoid this happening. For example, think about putting the positive side of yourself across. You might not have much work experience, but on the other hand you are young and energetic and keen to learn. There are also some simple rules to follow which should help you make the right impression.

Work in groups of three, with one person taking the role of interviewer, another that of the interviewee and the third acting as observer. Choose one of the following topics and carry out a five-minute interview on the subject.

1 Part-time or holiday jobs you have done.

2 What you remember about your primary school.

3 Your experiences as a trainee. What have you learnt? What have you found helpful and what do you think could be improved?

4 Your course at college (suggestions as for 3).

5 Your favourite way of spending a weekend.

6 Your last year at school.

7 Your proudest achievement.

8 Your favourite holiday.

Afterwards, the observer in your group should lead a discussion on how the interview went on both sides. Use the 'Suggestions for Interviewers and Interviewees' (below and overleaf) as check-lists for your discussion.

It's worth saying again that it really helps to be positive about yourself. Stress the good parts of your experience, not the bad ones. People are generally more impressed by hearing about the things you have learnt than by moans about how things went wrong. But if you can show how you have benefited from a bad experience then it can be a good idea to say so. For example, if you didn't do too well in maths exams at school, don't say 'I've always failed maths', but something like 'I used to do badly in maths, but since I've been working at X I've found it much easier. Now there seems to be some point in it. At school it never meant anything.' If you still find numbers impossible, try not to mention it!

Suggestions for interviewers

- Keep things going – prompt if the interviewee gets shy. e.g. 'And you enjoyed that? What else did you like?'
- Ask *open questions*, not ones that just require a 'yes' or 'no' answer. e.g. 'What was the best part of the job?' rather than 'Did you enjoy that job?'

- Try to ask follow-up questions. e.g. 'And how often did you have to do that?'
- Listen carefully to the answers so that you can choose the next question well.
- Remember to *look* encouraging and to smile.
- Open and close the interview pleasantly. i.e. greet the person, put them at their ease and thank them at the end.

Suggestions for interviewees

- Make the best of yourself. Concentrate on your achievements and don't be negative about your weaker points.
- Answer questions as fully as you can. Not just with 'yes' or 'no'.
- Don't go on and on. Keep your answers relevant and don't talk too fast.
- If you don't understand a question ask for it to be rephrased or repeated.
- If you don't want to answer a personal question, be tactful about it. Explain why without getting upset. For example, if you don't want to answer a question about whether you live at home, say something like: 'Things are a bit complicated at the moment. But I shan't have any trouble getting to work.'
- Try not to be nervous. Remember that interviewers can be shy too. Deep breaths can help before you go in.
- Catch the interviewer's eye so that you can judge his or her response to what you are saying.
- Remember to smile from time to time. People would rather work with a cheerful person than a miserable one. However, don't overdo it and start giggling.
- The way you move and sit also makes an impression. Try not to fidget too much; look relaxed but interested (but don't sprawl back in the chair). Try not to look down at your feet as you come into the room.

7.9 'I'd Like to Ask You . . . ?'

Interview someone who does the kind of job you'd like to do. Most people like to talk about themselves and should be pleased to give help and information to a young person. Discuss with the rest of the class the kind of questions you should ask, but try to cover some or all of the following topics:

1 Describing their work.
2 The kind of training they did.
3 How the training has or hasn't been useful.
4 Would they do the training differently if they were in charge? How would they do it?
5 The other people at work.
6 Do they all get on well?
7 What kind of facilities do they have, e.g. canteen, social club?
8 Is it a satisfying job? Why?
9 If they could change the job in any way, how would they do it?
10 How much recognition by employers for good work?
11 Promotion prospects.
12 Holidays; working hours; shift-work.

Remember not to stick rigidly to your questions; if something interesting is said, then follow it up. For example, if your interviewee says 'the one thing I don't like about driving a cab is the other drivers', then you could ask something like 'Why? What sort of thing do they do?'

If you can, you should tape the interview and analyse afterwards what went well and what could have gone better.

7.10 Guidelines

To sum up, here are some guidelnes on what to remember about making an impression:

– *be positive* about what you have to say. Stress the good sides, not the bad ones.

– if you're selling something, think of its *benefits* to your customer.

– *deal with objections* by turning them to your advantage.

– weigh up what your customer (or interviewer) *wants and needs.*

– think about the *kind of customer* you've got.

– *be enthusiastic* without overdoing it.

– try to *imagine what the other person is feeling.*

– remember to *smile and be pleasant* even if you're nervous.

Extended Exercise – Odd Job Agency

Choose one of the following activities and plan how to convince a potential customer to employ you. Then tape what you would say to them. Remember to include answers to objections that might be raised. For example, if you plan to be a baby-sitter you might be asked: 'Why should I pay you £1.50 an hour? I only gave £1 an hour to the last one.' And you should ideally be able to forestall that question.

Odd jobs

1 Doing shopping for another family.

2 Cleaning the inside and outside of a smart car.

3 Baby-sitting.

4 Cleaning a house.

5 Cleaning windows.

6 Painting and decorating.

7 Looking after a shop during the lunch hour.

8 Being a DJ at your local club.

9 Writing a sports report for your local paper.

10 Walking a dog.

11 Taking the photos at someone's wedding.

12 Making clothes or curtains.

13 Any other skill that you feel you have to offer.

8

Putting Your Case

8.1 Can I Have a Pay Rise?

The small boy pleading for a bar of chocolate in the supermarket – 'I *will* eat my lunch, Mummy, please. I'll pay for it myself out of next week's pocket money. *Please*,' – is making a case for what he wants. In the same way, we can put a case for anything from an end to fox-hunting to a pay rise. The small boy had the right idea. He'd got together what points he could muster – lunch and pocket money – to meet the objections he expected. And that's the first stage involved in putting a case; think of as many persuasive arguments as you can. For example, the case for a pay rise might go something like this:

1 I've been here six months.

2 I was promised a pay rise after six months.

3 People seem happy with my work. Mrs X said to me the other day that I was a real help – things had been easier since I arrived.

4 I've learnt how to do all the jobs in the office/workshop. (Give examples.)

5 I've got quite a lot of responsibilities – more than an ordinary trainee.

6 I do the same work as X who earns more than I do.

7 I'm moving out of home next week and I'm going to need the money.

Which of these arguments would you put first? The fact that you want or need a pay rise isn't enough of an argument, although it is reasonable to say why you need the extra money. You need to show your employer how useful you are; he or she doesn't want to have to train someone else if you leave. Incidentally it's also a good idea when asking for a pay rise to get help from your union, if you belong to one.

8.2 'It was the Buses'

Obviously it's not simply a question of finding some good arguments and throwing a list at the person you're trying to persuade. You've got to take the other person into account. What's the best way to approach the subject? Should you tackle it in a roundabout way or go straight to the main point? Which argument is this person going to find most persuasive? Should you begin with that or save it till the end? And most important, what tone should you use? Should you smile and flatter? Be thoughtful and see their point of view? Be loud and aggressive? Keep nagging away at the subject? Be brisk and businesslike? Or what? Listen to Tape Extract 30. Why do you think the incident ended disastrously for both parties?

TAPE EXTRACT 30

8.3 Friendly Persuasion 1

Work out what arguments you'd use if you had to deal with the following situations. You should come up with a list of points for each of them that looks something like the case for a pay rise outlined in 8.1.

1 Your college is holding a Rag Week festival to collect money for charity. One of the ideas is for a race through the centre of town. Students would wear silly costumes and carry banners advertising Rag Week events. You've been asked to get permission for the race from the local police.

2 You want to go on holiday with a group of friends. This is the first time you'd be going away without your parents and also the first time you'd miss the family holiday. Your parents are a bit doubtful about some of your friends, though not all of them.

3 You want some time off work to go to your brother's wedding which is being held at the other end of the country on a Friday. Your employer is not very sympathetic to people's private problems.

4 You want to leave home to share a flat with friends. You've got a job and your parents know the people you want to share with. However, they think you're still too young to live away from home.

5 Your friend wants to leave college early and get a job. You think this is a bad idea and you try to persuade him/her not to go.

6 You are a government trainee working for a private company. You like the job and the people. The company is a small one and takes on few new employees. You would like to be taken on as a permanent employee when you finish your training.

7 Your neighbours tend to play their stereo extremely loudly late at night. They leave windows open and have a lot of visitors who talk loudly and make a noise when they leave, often at 3 or 4 o'clock in the morning. You have to leave for work at 7.30 and are trying to study in the evenings, so their racket is quite disturbing. You like the neighbours, who are very friendly people, so you don't want a row. However, you do want something done about all this.

8.4 Friendly Persuasion 2

Read the advice section below, then, working with a partner choose one of the situations given in 8.3 and argue your case. You should take into account the kind of person(s) you're talking to. Think carefully about the best way to approach the subject.

Advice on putting arguments

- Put yourself in the other person's place. If you were them, what would persuade you?
- Think of the objections the other side might raise. Find answers and use these as part of your argument.
- Decide on what tone will be most effective with the person you need to persuade. Should you be formal or informal, charming or businesslike . . . ?
- Don't get angry if you're not getting anywhere. It might need time for your arguments to sink in. Aggression will only make things worse.
- Repeat any arguments that seem to have had an effect.

8.5 Making a Complaint

One of the occasions when you have to put a good case *and* keep a hold on your temper is when you're making a complaint. The facts are usually quite clear cut; you know why you're complaining. But it's important to organise what you have to say so that the other side doesn't get the edge on you. If they say they don't understand what you're talking about, you're immediately on the defensive and at a disadvantage, which is not what you want.

Try out one of the complaints we've outlined on pages 86–87. Work with a partner, who should try to make things difficult for you – in real life that's probably what would happen; few people are ready to admit they're in the wrong straight away. Before you start, read through the section below on 'Making a Complaint'.

Making a complaint

- Make a list of all your facts, including dates, prices, make of product if relevant.
- Make sure you speak to the right person; it won't help to say everything to an assistant who can't make a decision. Say that you want to speak to the manager because you have a complaint.
- Know what you want, e.g. replacement of goods, money back, free service.
- Know what you're entitled to: read the extract on the law given below. You can get further information on particular topics from the Citizens Advice Bureau.

1 What the law says

When you buy something you and the seller make a contract. Even if all you do is talk! The seller – not the manufacturer – must sort out your complaint.

The law has three rules:

1. Goods must be **of merchantable quality.** This means they must be reasonably fit for their normal purpose. Bear in mind the price and how the item was described. A new item must not be broken or damaged. It must work properly. But if it is very cheap, secondhand or a 'second' you cannot expect top quality.
2. Goods must be **as described** – on the package, a display sign or by the seller. Shirtsleeves should not be long if marked 'short' on the box. Plastic shoes should not be called leather.
3. Goods must be **fit for any particular purpose** made known to the seller. If the shop says a glue will mend china, then it should.

All goods—including those bought in sales—are covered (food too) if bought from a trader. For example, from shops, in street markets, through mail order catalogues or from door-to-door sellers.

– Don't be put off. If they refuse to do anything, say you'll get in touch with Head Office if they've got one. Or say that you'll write to the local paper or report them to the Council.

– Don't be side-tracked. They may try to use technical jargon or waffle. For example, 'Well, sir/madam, if there's a fault in the capiscular mechanism or the rear solid-state solinoid discs, you can't expect anything else, can you?' Or they may try flattery, 'A clever girl like you could easily mend that little tear, couldn't you?'

– Don't get angry. Keep calm and stick to the facts. Be pleasant but quite firm about what you want.

"Excuse me, but I'm afraid I've got a complaint"

1 You bought a pair of shoes last week, wore them once and they fell to bits. The manager asks where you wore them and then says that the shoes weren't made with that sort of treatment in mind. He says he can't do anything for you. He tries to suggest you bought them in a sale and that therefore they can't be exchanged. When you insist, he says he'll send them back to the manufacturer. However, you know that it is the shop's responsibility to put matters right.

about buying things

If things go wrong...

If there is something wrong with what you buy tell the seller at once. If any of the three rules have been broken you may be able to:

get a cash payment to make up the difference between what you paid and the reduced value of the faulty item, *or*

reject it and get your money back.

If you both agree, you may get a replacement or free repair.

Exactly what you are entitled to depends on how serious the fault is and how soon you tell the seller.

You are not entitled to anything if you:

- examined the item when you bought it and should have seen the faults
- were told about the faults
- simply change your mind about wanting it
- did the damage yourself
- got it as a present (the *buyer* must make the claim)

2 A second hand car which you bought from a local dealer stopped when you were on the motorway. The AA say its a write-off and unroadworthy. You paid £300 for it only three weeks ago. You've got a letter from the AA to prove your point and you want your money back. When the dealer protests, you point out that it's an offence under the Road Traffic Act to sell an unroadworthy car and that if he doesn't give you your money back you'll tell the police.

3 You bought a record yesterday from your local store. When you first played it you noticed that it had a bad scratch on it which looked as if it had been there for some time. The manager is reluctant to give you a new one but you point out that everyone you know buys records at the shop and you'll tell them what's happened and ask them to pass the word on.

4 Your motorbike has just been in for repair and when you are riding it home you notice that it is making a funny noise. You go back to the garage and ask them to fix it. When you say you want to know exactly what they did during the service, the manager replies that they don't keep records of that sort of thing and if you're not satisfied you can go elsewhere.

5 You come back from a package holiday with some friends. Neither the hotel nor

the place were anything like the description given in the brochure (see below). You go to see the tour operator who protests that everyone else who has gone on that holiday has enjoyed it.

> X *is* Greece. Full of charm, drenched with hot sun throughout the summer months, X offers first-class beaches, charming tavernas for that restful restina, opportunities for all kinds of entertainment, from donkey rides to dry skiing. Perfect for the young person in search of an active, exciting holiday. Nestling in the middle of the perfect Greek village, the hotel provides luxurious facilities as well as typical Greek hospitality.

8.6 Fact or Opinion?

When you're putting a case which someone else is likely to argue with, it's important to be clear about whether you're making an objective statement or a subjective one. For example, if you say '*Coronation Street* is about boring people talking about boring things in a boring place', you're making a subjective statement. It's your opinion, and someone else may or may not agree with it. But '*Coronation Street* is a script-writer's view of how people live in a Northern town' is an objective statement of fact. Pick out from the list below which are facts and which are opinions.

a) Trees are beautiful.
b) Spring is one of the seasons of the year.
c) Britain is a multi-racial country.
d) Babies get nappy rash.
e) Garage mechanics do a dirty job.
f) Newsapapers are biased.
g) Children like playing with toys.
h) Clocks tell the time.
i) People who smoke tend to get lung cancer more often than people who don't.
j) More than 90% of British households have a television.
k) Tapes are better than records.
l) Make-up makes women look prettier.
m) Sport is good for you.
n) The 1984 Olympics were held in Los Angeles.
o) Oranges contain Vitamin C.

8.7 Supporting Evidence

When you're putting your case it's useful to have some objective information to support your subjective arguments. And if you can't always manage statistics, you can usually find examples from your own experience. For example, if you were making the case that there is discrimination in the employment of women, you might point to the fact that none of the people in high positions in your college is a woman.

Choose some of the examples from the list of opinions below and see if you can find some facts from your own experience which prove or disprove the arguments.

a) Cats make better pets than dogs.
b) Only mindless people watch TV.
c) Computers put people out of work.
d) Only women like babies.
e) Men can't cook.
f) Reading novels is boring.
g) Being in debt is always bad.
i) Being a trainee is a waste of time.
j) You can rely on your friends more than you can on your family.
k) Taking drugs does you harm.

8.8 Useful Phrases

It can help to have a set of useful phrases to help express the evidence you're using to support your arguments. For example:

'I think X is wrong because . . .' then give your fact or illustration or statistic.

'The main reasons in favour of/against X are . . .' then give a brief list of points.

'It could be argued that X is so. This is not the case because . . .' then give reasons, illustrations etc.

'Although many people think that X is so, I disagree because . . .' Give reasons, illustrations etc.

'To sum up, I think X should happen/is so because . . .' Repeat your main reasons and illustraions.

Using some of the examples from this list, put your case either for or against one of the opinions given in Section 8.7.

8.9 Guidelines

To sum up, here are some guidelines to use when you're putting your case:

- *collect together all the arguments* for your case.
- *put yourself in the other person's place*: if you were them, what would persuade you?
- *think of the objections* the other side might raise. Find answers and use them as part of your argument.
- *repeat any arguments* that seem to have had an effect.
- *don't get angry* if you're not getting anywhere.
- *decide on what tone* will be most effective for the person you need to persuade.
- make sure you *know any necessary facts.*

– *don't let the other side put you off by flattering you or using technical language you don't understand.*

– make sure you are clear about *the difference between opinion and fact.*

– *use illustrations from your own experience* to support the points you make.

Extended Exercise – Putting Your Case

Each person in the group should make a case either for or against one of the following topics. Supporting material on topic 1 is given on pages 91–93:

1 Children are brainwashed into being stereotyped boys and girls.

2 The slaughter of seals and whales and of animals for fur should be stopped.

3 All experiments on live animals should cease (see pp. 6–7).

4 Exams should be abolished.

5 Disabled people should be integrated into jobs, schools, social life etc.

6 Fox hunting should be banned.

7 Britain should become a non-nuclear nation immediately.

8 There should be random tests on all athletes in Britain for drug use. They should be disqualified from representing their country for life if found out.

9 Cigarette companies should be prevented by law from sponsoring sporting events.

10 Football clubs should face automatic relegation if their fans are found to have caused trouble.

11 Young people should form a political pressure group to gain support for issues that particularly concern them.

12 Doctors should always treat what patients tell them in strict confidence. The age of the patient should make no difference to them.

13 The age of consent should be lowered.

14 The school leaving age should be raised to 18.

15 The government should set up many more centres to provide help for people with drug or alcohol problems.

How girls learn to be women

Reading primers usually focus on a family, especially the children and their activities. They are meant to seem 'normal', and because of this, they present people who are exaggerated and even caricatured: for instance mothers who seldon go outside the home and never have any sort of job, and working class women with hair tied up in Mrs-Mop-style scarves.

Looking more closely at the parts played by girls and women, it becomes clear that they are cast as the passive supporting characters for their vigorous male counterparts. 'Mummy' seems to have a particularly dull time—all her life revolves around servicing 'daddy' and the children by preparing food and making beds, by cleaning, washing and ironing, with sewing and knitting as her leisure activities. When she ventures outside the home, it is only to 'shop'. 'Daddy' is the pampered breadwinner. He is the person who goes off into the unseen outside world, and who eventually also returns from it. He will never be seen washing or making beds. He is the one who drives the car, paints the house and plays with the children, especially with Peter. In his leisure time he also reads the newspaper, a pastime in which 'mummy' shows little apparent interest.

The different characteristics for boys and girls are implicitly endorsed. Little girls are good, sweet, quiet and thoroughly angelic, and they like helping mother in the home. Boys are not expected to behave like this and are seldom involved with anything very domestic. It is their prerogative to be naughty, which is assumed to come naturally with being a boy. When brother and sister are portrayed doing things together, the boy is clearly the active, commanding and dominating figure, while the girl is a pliant and passive observer. For example, Jane has to watch Peter make a sandcastle, a go-cart, a doll's house. At his command she watches him: 'Look at me Jane, look at me in the boat.' If Jane asks to join in when Peter is playing with his toy train and station, then she must obey his orders: "Yes," says Peter, "I have the train. You play with the station." And Jane always obeys. When they are seen with their parents, they imitate appropriately. 'Peter helps daddy with the car and Jane helps mummy with the tea.' 'Jane wants to make cakes like mummy.' '"I will be the man in the shop," says Peter. "Then let me be mummy," says Jane.' Girls only seem to show any active spirit when they are given the opportunity to help mummy with the dusting, sweeping and polishing, or pretending to prepare tea.

It is often the pictures as much as the written sentences that impress readily absorbable images on minds and imaginations. It is the illustrations too that tend to go even further than the words. The method of teaching that uses a technique of 'Look and Say' is frequently used, and relies heavily on pictured interpretations. A short and simple sentence is illustrated by a colourful and detailed drawing showing the words in action. For instance, a sentence such as 'Here we are dressing up' would be accompanied by an illustration in which girls and boys are seen donning the grab of traditional feminine and masculine characters, or possible future roles. Boys put on costumes of cowboys, policemen, firemen, while girls are dressing as princesses, nurses and brides. Toys that are pictured also follow the traditional roles. Girls have the inevitable doll, while boys play with cars, boats, planes and trains. The innocence of a sentence 'Peter has a toy and Jane has a toy' is soon lost in its interpretation.

Peter and Jane are at home.

They want to make a car to play with. They want to make a car like Daddy's.

Jane helps Peter. "It looks good," she says. "We can have fun with it."

"I want to make it red," says Peter.

"Yes," says Jane, "we can make it red. You and I like red."

new words
make she

Jane likes to help Mummy. She wants to make cakes like Mummy.

"Let me help you, Mummy," she says. "Will you let me help, please? I can make cakes like you."

"Yes," says Mummy, "I will let you help me. You are a good girl."

"We will make some cakes for Peter and Daddy," says Jane. "They like the cakes we make."

new words
Let let will

The bold experiment to raise nonsexist children is not working. Boys are not dressing baby dolls. Girls are not playing with trucks. This problem is baffling those who have devoted themselves to eradicating sexism and sex stereotypes in their families. "The most important thing you can do," claims one woman executive, "is to change your own role models. Sometimes my husband cooks, sometimes I do; sometimes he fixes the toys, sometimes I do. We each are careful to spend a great deal of time alone with the children, and we both work less than full time in order to be home with them. But when my son came to visit my office, it took hours to convince him that my staff worked for me and not for Daddy."

Jenny, whose mother is a doctor, believes only boys can be doctors. She plays at being a nurse. Sarah's parents are both full-time professionals. When she grows up, she plans to be a bride, or maybe a princess. Four-year-old Ned explains what men are like: They build houses, they are the boss and the president.

Sara Stein, *Girls and Boys: The Limits of Non-Sexist Childrearing*

9

Under Discussion

9.1 Tricks in Argument

Arguments or discussions are rarely one-sided. Few people will stand back, shut up and let you put your case in your own way. They want their say. They want to persuade *you*. So if you're to answer their arguments, you've got to listen carefully and learn how to answer the points they make. People often use tricks when they're arguing – though they usually don't know that that's what they're doing. It's useful to know about some of these tricks as it's easy to be persuaded by impressive-sounding arguments which don't make so much sense when you look at them more closely.

Here's a list of the kind of tricks you might find used in arguments. As you go through them, try to think of other examples you have come across.

1 Wild generalisation

What to look out for: words like 'all' or 'always'.
e.g. 'All young men on motorbikes are a dangerous menace.'
or 'Young people today are a lot of lazy layabouts.'

2 Going to absurd lengths to prove a point

What to look out for: a long list of unlikely consequences.
e.g. 'You'll fall off your bike, break your back, lose your job, get chucked out of your flat and then where'll you be?'

3 Referring to a possibly doubtful authority

What to look out for: 'So and so said it was true.'
e.g. 'The local paper said all the shops would close if we had a supermarket' (so it must be true)
or 'My father votes for X; he says he's a good politician' (so X must be all right)

4 Trying to impress by name dropping

What to look out for: famous names in unlikely contexts.
e.g. 'John McEnroe uses this kind of razor so you should too.' (He's a top tennis star, not necessarily a shaving expert.)

5 Evasion – or changing the subject when arguments get tricky

What to look out for: waffle, or a statement that just doesn't follow.
e.g. 'Well, none of that really matters, does it? Not when you really get down to it. You know what I mean.'
or 'Of course, she's got such lovely hair', when you've been discussing her chances of promotion.

6 Putting words into your mouth

What to look out for: 'in other words you're saying'
e.g. *A*: 'We need a good rubbish disposal system'
B: 'In other words you're saying it should be put out to private contractors.'

7 Linking statements that do not follow

What to look out for: statements on the same subject which aren't really connected.
e.g. 'Cars are dangerous. Look at the number of people who drive badly.'

8 Misuse of statistics

What to look out for: figures included to try and impress – but usually unsupported by evidence.
e.g. 'Seventy-eight per cent of people questioned preferred Brand X margarine' (to what? Butter? Brand Y margarine? Candle wax?)

9 Distorting facts or plain lying

What to look out for: inconsistency or unlikely stores.
e.g. 'This coffee machine can make thirty cups of coffee in an hour.' (Only if you spend most of that hour filling it up with water, emptying the filters, washing the jug etc.)

10 Resorting to abuse, anger, temper or even violence

What to look out for: abandonment of reasonable argument, shouting.
e.g. 'Rubbish'; 'Balls'; 'That's stupid.'

11 Using false or misleading comparisons

What to look out for: any comparison which tries to prove a point – though not all comparisons are misleading.

e.g. 'If Mary can pass her driving test first time, so can you.' (But Mary has been learning longer, has had more practice and is five years older.)

12 Blinding with science

What to look out for: a lot of technical terms which don't directly bear on the argument.

e.g. 'Of course your sort of music's all right, but it doesn't have the cadences and subtle rhythmic legato of some of Shostakovitch's melodies.'

13 Persuader words

What to look our for: 'Surely'; 'obviously'; 'of course'.

e.g. Surely it's obvious that everybody must have some kind of religious belief.'

14 Emotive words

What to look out for: words which make uproved judgements

e.g. 'In Spain earlier today freedom fighters attacked an army convoy. Two soldiers were killed.' 'Earlier today terrorists murdered two soldiers in Southern Spain.'

15 Lump in the throat technique

What to look out for: pathetic descriptions designed to make your feelings overcome your reason.

e.g. 'Row upon row of sad white bodies waiting for the torturer's needle' (about a group of white rats being used for medical experiment).

16 Personal attack in place of reasoned argument

What to look out for: personal abuse which is designed to take your mind off the argument.

e.g. 'You would be against war, you're a coward.'

or 'Decent honest people believe that our countryside should be protected.'

Listen to Tape Extract 31. Try to pick out some of the tricks the second speaker is using. How could you have dealt with him differently?

TAPE EXTRACT 31

9.2 Personal Remarks in Arguments

If you want to 'play dirty' and distract the other side from its arguments, make a personal remark. Drag an insult or compliment into the discussion and you'll find the other person will probably react to the remark and forget about the argument. For example, when a woman presenter on the radio asked a famous BBC interviewer an awkward question he answered something like this: 'What I don't understand is why a beautiful woman like you wants to do a job like this.' What he hoped was that the presenter would immediately be flustered by the compliment (or apparent compliment), forget about her original question and answer what he had said. In fact she quite determinedly pressed on with what she was saying.

Compliments are off-putting, but so are direct insults. What would you say if the middle-aged man you were talking to quite politely about the difficulties young people face in the job market suddenly turned round and said this: 'Of course, I'd never give a job to anyone who looked like you.' Here are some possible reactions. Which do you think would be the best ones to use?

1 Slap his face or punch him on the nose.

2 Walk out.

3 Insult him back. ('I think your suit smells of mothballs'.)

4 Ask him *why* he wouldn't employ you.

5 Point out that you are perfectly clean and tidy.

6 Ask why he wears a suit to work.

7 Ask if he's ever asked his customers or other people in the office whether they object to your sort of fashion.

8 Suggest that he might be being a bit old-fashioned.

9 Say that actually he would look really sweet if he was a bit more modern in the way he dressed.

10 Point out that the way *you* dress is beside the point – the argument was about young people's prospects of employment.

Ways of dealing with insults and personal remarks

– Don't get angry. You've lost the argument if you lose control.

– If the insult is designed to drag you away from the main argument, point out politely that what has been said is not on the subject. You could say something like: 'We're discussing X and you seem to have got off the subject.' or 'That's irrelevant, what we're discussing is. . . '

9.3 Coping with Insults

Some insulting behaviour isn't directly related to an argument. It just turns up in the course of people's lives. However, it's just as important to deal with it properly – for your own self-esteem if nothing else. Listen to Tape Extract 32. Do you think the customer reacted properly?

TAPE EXTRACT 32

Choose some of the examples of insults in the situations given below and work out how you would react if they happened to you.

1 You take a message to another office for your employer. They keep you waiting for twenty minutes for an answer and don't even ask if you'd like to sit down.

2 You go for a job interview and before they even start asking you any questions they say something like 'We wanted someone older. We're not really interested in school leavers.'

3 You are with a group of friends in a pub, not making much noise, just having a good time. A couple get up to leave and as they pass your table the woman says loudly 'You've only got to look at them. No wonder they can't get a job. Lazy, half-witted and dishonest as well, I shouldn't wonder.'

4 You're introduced to your boy or girlfriend's ex. He or she takes one look, turns

to a friend and says 'You'd think he (or she) could have found something a bit better than that, wouldn't you?'

9.4 Bias and Prejudice

Another kind of situation which is hard to deal with occurs when people make biased or prejudiced statements about whole groups. You may not belong to the group which is being attacked, but you may be offended on their behalf. How would you cope with these statements?

1 'Of course, they're all nutters. A load of loonies. Ought to be locked up. They used to have Bedlams where they could dump anyone who was round the bend. Good idea. I don't want people like that living down the road. You don't know what they'll do next. Can't have them wandering around loose in the streets.'

2 (Spoken in the same room as someone in a wheelchair) 'I'm terribly sorry for them. I know handicapped people have a terrible time. It's very hard being different. Not able to run about and enjoy life. Must be dreadful. Here's the tea, dear. Does he take sugar?'

3 'Of course women are as clever as men. I wouldn't say they weren't for a moment. They're just good at different things, that's all. They're more emotional, more sensitive, more caring. And that can get in the way of rational decisions. I mean, let's face it, when a woman tries to act like a man she just ends up being a bitch, doesn't she? No, the old ways are the best.'

4 'They're different. Nothing against them. It's just that they're different. They wear funny clothes and eat different food and they can't talk English properly and they've got an odd sort of religion. Some of them killed a sheep in the street the other day. What kind of behaviour is that, eh? It's not the sort of thing we do. I wish they'd all go home. This country's changed so much I just don't recognise it.'

One of the ways of dealing with this kind of situation is to ask some polite but pointed questions. For example, with (1) you could say something like: 'Do you really want to keep someone who's mentally ill locked up with no chance of getting back to a normal life?' This should have the effect of making your prejudiced speaker at least argue some of his/her points; up to now they've just been making unsupported assertions, not arguments. The other thing you've done is to point out gently that you don't like the terms, 'loonies' or 'nutters' – as far as you're concerned you're talking about *people*. This should make it harder for the other person to make quite such sweeping statements. It's easier to be cruel to 'loonies' than to people who are ill. A campaign by the Down's Children's Association worked on this same point. The two ads printed below and opposite are a good illustration of how to deal with prejudice. What do you think makes them effective?

Don't say "Mongol".

Why?

It's offensive

—parents, and even some Down's people themselves, have said they would prefer a term which does not sound like some sort of half-breed dog.

It's hopelessly inaccurate

—the Victorian doctor who identified the syndrome (Dr. Langdon Down) thought the handicap resulted from a throwback to 'inferior races'. He coined the term 'Mongolian Idiots'. Variations he called 'Negroid Idiots', 'Aztec Idiots', 'Malaysian Idiots'—but none of these has entered the language.

The 'inferior race' theory was a wretched notion, and it was **wrong**. The cause is a genetic accident. It can happen to any couple and does happen to 1,000 families in Britain every year.

It conveys the wrong image

—'Mongol' is a Victorian word and conjures up a picture of the institutional lunatics of the time. Our children are nearly all brought up in ordinary families where a much greater potential for development is realised. Most will walk and talk, many will read and write and can look forward to a semi-independent adult life in sheltered accommodation, able to make real choices about their own lives.

9.5 Angry Resident

On most occasions prejudice doesn't come right out into the open and it's hard to deal with it directly. However, sometimes it can be coped with constructively, particularly if you don't get too personally involved, and if you try to see the other person's point of view. Take this example of a letter written to a local newspaper by residents angry about a new 16–19 college which has opened at the end of their road.

ANGRY RESIDENTS PROTEST - STUDENT BEHAVIOUR 'INTOLERABLE'

Sir,

On two occasions since Rudwick College opened you have given front page reports on the chaotic conditions prevailing there...

But whilst chaos and upheaval reigns in the college, what of the chaos and noise that local residents are subjected to? Cars are parked on the pavement, and, still worse, on the pavements at street corners. The noise from motor cycles is such that at times conversation is impossible. To add to this, our streets are littered with paper, Coca Cola tins and empty milk bottles. Huge transistor radios are carried by students at all times of the day, blasting out music so loudly that babies wake and old people are unable to take their afternoon naps. All in all, we have found students' behaviour to be quite intolerable.

We appeal to students (whom we support financially via our local authority rates) to have some consideration for other people. And if the young people themselves won't listen to what we say, and we suspect they won't, then perhaps their parents should knock some sense into their heads.

Yours faithfully

John Smith

12 Gradge Crescent
Rudwick

A group of students has been asked by the students' union to go round and talk to the person who has sent the letter. Working in small groups, prepare together what you will say to Mr Smith; then act out the meeting, with someone taking the part of Mr Smith. You should take into account the following points:

1 There is evidence of litter on Gradge Crescent. However, not all of it is left by students. The milkman is responsible for some of the empty milk bottles; he has refused to take away bottles from another dairy and these have been left lying around.

2 Students must have some form of transport and the college authorities are refusing to allow student cars to be parked in the college car park. Planning permission for a larger car park has been held up.

3 No one has heard noise from the radios that were complained of. More information (on times of day noise is heard etc.) is needed.

Remember:

- Always be polite. If Mr Smith insults you, your politeness will only point up his rudeness.
- Make positive suggestions for improvement.
- Admit a limited amount of guilt where the facts support it.
- Ask him to get more information for you. This should make him feel that you are treating his complaints seriously.
- Be sure to make notes on what is agreed and at the end of the meeting go over them to make sure he agrees with the action to be taken. The notes can be used later if he tries to backslide.

9.6 Listening to and Responding to Arguments

When you're having a discussion about an issue, whatever that issue is, it's important to listen carefully to what is said by the other side.

There are a few useful techniques which help when you're answering another person's argument.

- Try to use humour. Making people laugh is a good way of getting them on your side.
- Use contrasts. For example: '*On one hand* you say that young people dress in a casual and untidy way, but *on the other hand* their way of dressing can have the effect of making contacts in business easier and less formal. And when people are relaxed they are likely to be better customers.' (This argument has many holes in it but it will do as an example.)
- Then there's the admission that they may be partly right. This disarms them, at which point you can produce your own strong argument. You could say something like: 'What you say is true to some extent, but on the other hand. . . '

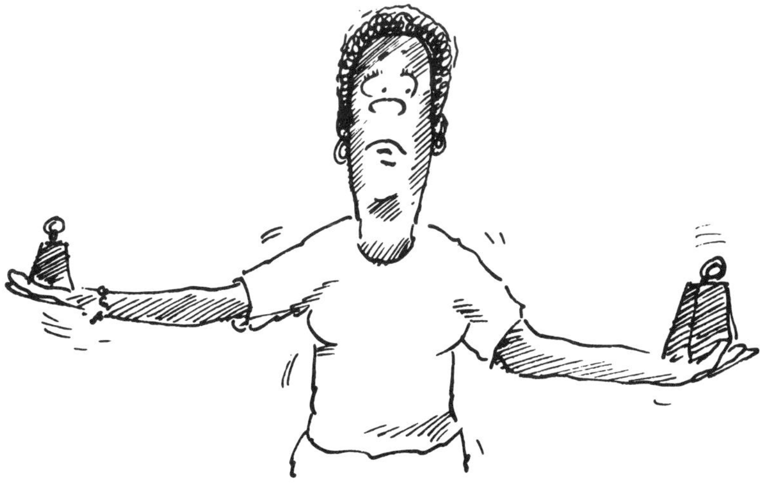

– There are also some useful ways of putting your disagreement with the other side. For example:

  – 'I don't agree with your argument because. . .' then give your facts, illustrations etc.

  – 'The information you've given is misleading/false because. . . ' then provide your own information.

  – 'You've tried to persuade us by suggesting X but this is a wild generalisation/ takes the argument ridiculously far etc.'

Choose one of the following topics that most people in the group agree is interesting. Then divide into two groups, each taking an opposite view. Then try to discuss the issue fully; treat the discussion like a kind of tennis match. If someone makes a point (e.g. 'all leopards have spots') then the next person has to follow that point up. (e.g. 'you say that all leopards have spots, but I know of two leopards which have only got blotches.') They can't just move on to another aspect of the subject. (e.g. 'male leopards are the hunters.') When they have followed the point up in some way then they are free to develop a different though related point. (e.g. 'so leopards aren't all the same and you can see that from the way they bring up their cubs. . .')

Suggested topics

1 'Anyone who smokes, takes drugs, sniffs glue or drinks too much is a stupid, self-destructive idiot.'

2 'Style is everything. It doesn't so much matter about jobs, money or ideas, as long as you're in fashion.'

3 'You can measure how successful a person is by how much money he or she earns.'

4 'Everybody should speak more than one language.'

5 'Everybody makes far too much fuss about the royal family.'

9.7 Guidelines

To sum up, here are some guidelines to use when you're having a discussion:

- *be aware of the kind of tricks* people can use in arguments.
- *don't get angry,* even if you're insulted.
- *get the other side back to the point* if they try to evade the argument.
- be ready to argue individual points in the other side's case by *using facts as well as opinions.*
- when people make prejudiced statements, *ask polite questions to make them argue their point of view*
- if possible, *try to see the other side's point of view.*
- always *try to be polite, but firm.*
- *use humour* where it seems appropriate. It can add to a good argument and helps to take away the sting of your disagreement.
- *use contrasts* in argument. "On the one hand. . . on the other hand. . . "
- *admit that your opponent may be partly right.* Then immediately produce an opposing strong argument of your own.
- *agree to disagree* if you know you can't change an opponent's point of view.

Extended Exercise – WCC versus BRAG and others

In this exercise, you have to argue the pros and cons of a realistic, though in this case fictional, road improvement scheme.

When you've read all the background information about the scheme itself, look at the sections 'How to Conduct the Meeting' (p. 109) and 'Who's at the Meeting' (p. 110–112). Then prepare your arguments and run the meeting, remembering to make use of the advice on pages 94–97.

After the meeting, either straight away or on a later occasion, members of the group should record a brief report of the meeting for Westchester Radio, conducting interviews with some of the speakers, and keeping a balanced overall impression for the *Roundabout Westchester* news magazine programme.

The story so far

Westchester City Council have announced in the local press road improvements which will affect the Bream area of the city. Local residents and traders are greatly worried about the scheme and many have contacted the council. The council's Highways Committee has offered to organise a public consultative meeting in Bream Community Centre to explain the scheme and hear views from local people.

Background information

Bream is a pleasant suburb of the city of Westchester. There is a ring road through the suburbs which takes traffic round Westchester, – keeping it away from the busy city centre.

Traffic on the ring road consists both of local vehicles and increasingly large numbers of heavy lorries carrying goods from Europe and wanting to get on to the motorway system going North and West. There are also many lorries taking materials and goods between the continental ports and the successful Westside Industrial Estate, which is engaged in heavy and light engineering. Lorries choose the southern section of the ring road where possible as the northern section is extremely awkward for large vehicles. (This is because the road narrows to two lanes near Westchester Station where it goes through a low bridge under the railway lines.)

The ring road as it passes through Bream is actually Bream High Street, which is a popular shopping street. This stretch of road is often very congested, creating a bottleneck in the ring road traffic flow and causing long delays.

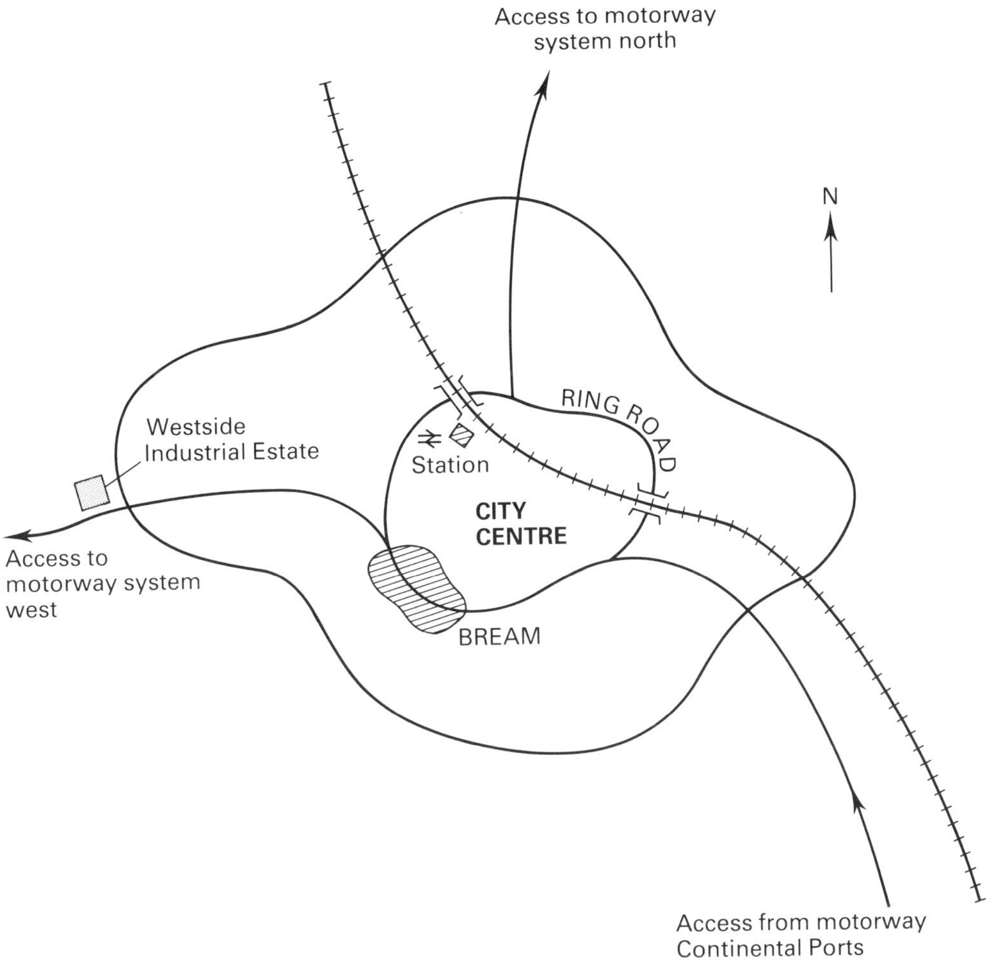

The improvement scheme

Westchester City Council, with backing from the Ministry of Transport, want to introduce a scheme to remove the problem of delays to traffic through Bream by:

a) widening the road to four lanes (presently three)
b) increasing speed limit from 30 to 40 m.p.h.
c) removing all road level pedestrian crossings and substituting foot-bridges
d) closing access from small side roads into main road
e) closing access to Primary School and supermarket car parks from main road
f) major junction alteration: Bream High Street/Bream Lane. This will involve moving the War Memorial to the Health Centre forecourt, and building an underpass for Bream Lane. 'The Bear' public house and several shops and houses will have to be demolished. Traffic access from Bream Lane to Bream High Street will be three-quarters of a mile away to the East at the Black Cross roundabout.

City Engineers Dept: Ring Road / Bream High Street

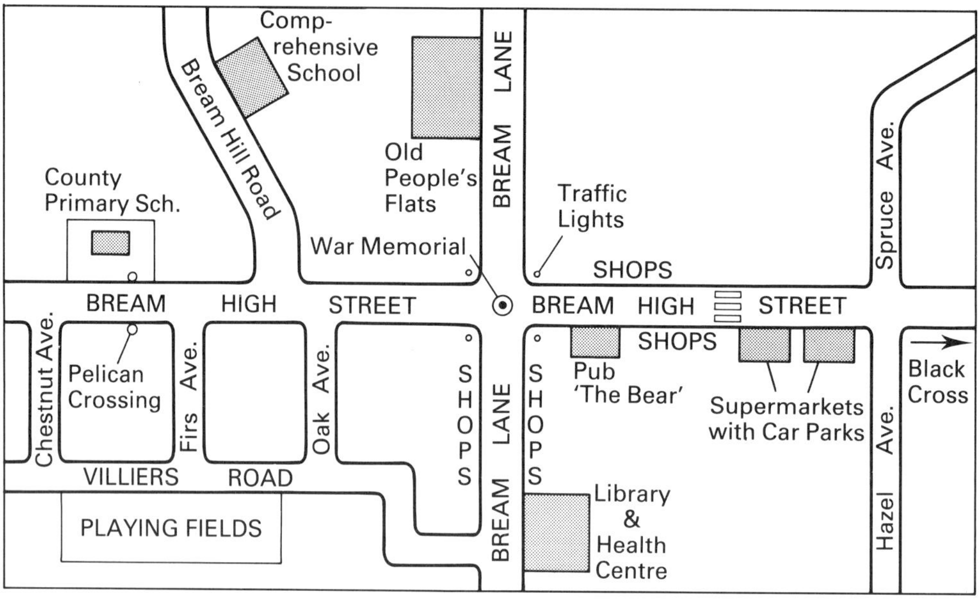

City Engineer's Dept: Ring Road / Bream High Street Improvement Scheme

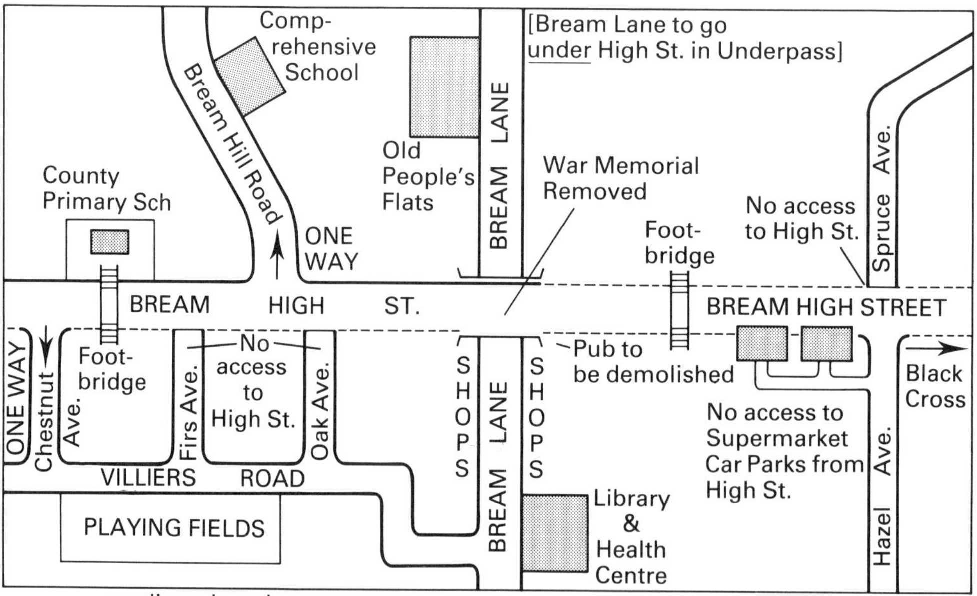

-------- re-aligned roadway
(i.e. reduced pavement width)

Everyone in the class should speak: the main speakers for about five minutes each, and the speakers from the audience for about two to three minutes each. The Chairperson should aim to keep the meeting under control and moving briskly. Follow the agenda below.

How to conduct the meeting

Members of the group take on the rôles of main speakers and audience at the public consultative meeting to discuss whether the Road Improvement Scheme should go ahead. Each speaker (apart from the Chairperson who must remain impartial) should argue persuasively for or against the scheme, trying to make everyone else agree.

Public Consultative Meeting on

Westchester City Council's proposals for a

BREAM HIGH ROAD IMPROVEMENT SCHEME

AGENDA

1. Chairperson's welcome and introduction to the purpose of the meeting
2. Introduction of the Platform Speakers
3. The Platform Speakers:
   (i) Westchester City Engineer
   (ii) Representative of BRAG: Bream Residents Action Group
   (iii) Manager, Westchester Bus Company
   (iv) Representative, Bream Chamber of Commerce
   (v) Representative, Road Hauliers Association
   (vi) Represent., Bream County Primary School, Parent Teachers Association
4. Views and Questions from audience
5. Summing-up of ideas:
   (i) Representative of BRAG
   (ii) Westchester City Engineer
6. Vote on feeling of meeting for or against the scheme
7. Chairperson's announcement of result of vote and closure of meeting.

Who's who at the meeting

Chairperson: Mayor of Westchester

The six platform speakers:

FOR	AGAINST
City Engineer	Rep. BRAG, Residents' Association
Manager, Westchester Bus Company	Rep. Bream Chamber of Commerce
Rep. Road Hauliers Association	Rep. Bream County Primary School Parent Teachers Association

Audience speakers

Commuter who drives to work on the Westside Industrial Estate from Bream and who resents the traffic jams	Matron of Old People's flats in Bream Lane
Resident of Oak Avenue who objects to his road being used as a 'rat-run' and welcomes restriction of access	Someone who feels the War Memorial, erected in 1919, should not be moved
Hospital administrator who feels that congestion is dangerous as it delays fire engines and ambulances	Landlord of 'The Bear' pub at junction of High St. and Bream Lane which would have to be demolished. The pub was built as a coaching inn and is a Bream landmark
Worker who travels by bus and is fed up with the long waits	Pupil at Bream Comprehensive who cycles to school and will have to go a long way round to get home
Taxi driver who is annoyed by traffic jams	Administrator of Health Centre in Bream Lane
Someone who lives near Westchester Station and would welcome relief from pressure on northern part of ring road	Manager of Topsave Supermarket (at present sited opposite zebra crossing)
Manager of small food-processing firm in Westside Industrial Estate who is anxious to speed up transport to and from the ports	Mother of three pre-school children who often has to cross the High Street
Resident who believes that Improvement Scheme represents progress	Owner of paper shop/tobacconist on High Street who is worried that his trade will fall off

Briefings: The Main Speakers Against the Scheme

2. Representative, Bream Residents Action Group

You represent the Action Group which was recently set up to fight the road scheme. You value the quality of life in Bream and want to keep it a pleasant place to live.
YOU ARE AGAINST THE SCHEME
a)The road will become a barrier dividing the community in half and destroying Bream's character.
b) The road will become like a race-track - noise, vibration and air pollution will increase.
c) Crossing the road by footbridge will be a nuisance to all, particularly the elderly, infirm and those with prams and pushchairs.
d) Local residents with cars, motor cycles and bicycles will have to make long detours to gain access to the road.
e) The value of houses and flats in Bream will fall as the area ceases to be a desirable one to live in.

4. Representative, Bream Chamber of Commerce

You represent local traders. Bream is a thriving local shopping area with shoppers coming more or less equally from both sides of the High Street.
YOU ARE AGAINST THE SCHEME
a) Shoppers will find it troublesome to cross the 'improved' road and so trade will suffer.
b)Shoppers in cars won't be able to park in side streets since access will be cut off - so they will drive on to other districts.
c) Narrow pavements and fast traffic will make shopping unpleasant and dangerous - especially for the elderly and those with young children.
d) Some shops may well lose so much trade that they will have to close and the appeal of the High Street as a shopping area will then rapidly deteriorate.

6. Representative, Bream County Primary School PTA

You represent the parents and teachers of children at the school. The school playground is alongside Bream High Street. Children come to your school from all over Bream, mainly on foot. The crossing is a Pelican-type, with a lollipop lady to help.
YOU ARE AGAINST THE SCHEME
a) The new road is a potential danger to the children - traffic will move much faster. (Probably at more than 40 mph, the proposed new limit).
b) The footbridge will be a nuisance, particularly for mothers with children in prams and pushchairs.
c) The school uses the playing fields in Villiers Road - access will be difficult.
d) Access to the school car-park will be closed. Expensive new access via Bream Hill Road will have to be organized by the Council and it will be more difficult to reach the school by road.

Briefings: The Main Speakers For the Scheme

1. City Engineer

You are responsible for all the detailed work on planning improvements to the Ring Road and reducing congestion in Bream. Your department has carried out a detailed analysis of traffic and feels that a drastic scheme is essential.
YOU ARE FOR THE SCHEME.
a) It is your responsibility to provide good modern roads which will be a credit to the city.
b) Traffic through Bream is extremely heavy, especially at peak hours. Congestion causes tail-backs into neighbouring districts.
c) The combination of heavy traffic and pedestrians is dangerous - it will be safer to restrict pedestrians to footbridges.
d) The High Street was built many years ago and was not designed to carry heavy traffic.
e) The improvements may initially cause opposition, but people will quickly appreciate advantages of being able to travel quickly and without delay.

3. Manager, Westchester Bus Company

You run the City Bus service, and Bream is a notorious bottleneck causing severe delays to all public transport.
YOU ARE FOR THE SCHEME
a) Buses will no longer get held up by the pedestrian crossings and at the intersection with Bream Lane.
b) The service will improve all along the Ring Road and will become more efficient - provoking fewer complaints.
c) When the service improves more people will use the buses in preference to their cars.
d) Slowly moving buses consume more fuel and make more fumes to pollute the air.

5. Representative, Road Hauliers Association

Your members drive large lorries and delivery vans through Westchester. The lorries are either travelling between the ports and the motorway system or serving the Westside Industrial Estate. The drivers find the delays in Bream a great nuisance.
YOU ARE FOR THE SCHEME
a) Delays cost your members money - these costs are passed on to the consumer as higher prices.
b) Local traffic from the side roads and going in and out of car parks cause lorries to brake suddenly risking accidents.
c) Pedestrians are safer off ground level away from risk of road injury.
d) Your lorries are trying to cross the city as quickly as possible. The route round the north side of the Ring Road is even more difficult. (See Background Information).
e) The Westside Industrial Estate is important to Westchester's prosperity and employment. It needs efficient road access.

Appendix One
Information on guests for 'The Seagull Retreat'

1 *Mr Kleghart* from Austria, travelling with his wife and small baby. He wants to stay for a week. He arrives on Monday, September 12th at 2.30 p.m. and plans to leave the following Sunday in the morning. He wants a quiet room with a bath and half board, also a cot for the baby. His English is not very good, although he thinks it is and gets annoyed if misunderstood.

2 *M Hulot* from France, travelling on business. He wants a room with half board and is not bothered by the view. However, he does like to have a bath in the morning. He arrives on Monday, September 12th at 5 p.m. and will be leaving on Friday morning at 8.00 a.m. sharp, so he'd like an early breakfast at 7.00 a.m. He flirts with the receptionist if she's female.

3 *Ms Catchpole,* travelling alone, wishes to stay for three nights from Wednesday, September 14th to Friday, September 16th inclusive. She arrives at 3 p.m. on the Wednesday and plans to leave on Saturday morning at about 11.00 a.m. She wants a room with a shower and only bed and breakfast. She's particularly fond of fresh air and loves to look at the sea at night. She's rather shy and nervous and doesn't always speak very clearly.

4 *Ms Smythe,* travelling with a Mr Howes for a few days holiday. She wants a double room with a shower, bed and breakfast only. They arrive on Thursday, September 15th at 11.00 a.m. and expect to leave on Sunday 18th in the afternoon. She and Mr Howes want to be quiet and undisturbed by children, but they would like a view of the sea. She is rather brisk and businesslike and tends to be impatient.

5 *Mrs Bryant,* travelling with her husband and another couple, the Stevensons, arrives on Saturday afternoon to enquire whether you could fit them in for two nights bed and breakfast. They expect to leave after breakfast on Monday, September 19th. Ideally both couples would like a bath and a sea-view, but at such short notice they'd settle for whatever you can offer. She is very keen to stay as she thinks Pebbleton a lovely little place. She is very chatty.

Appendix Two
Bank Managers Loan Tables

Personal Loan

REPAYMENT TABLES

How to use the Repayment Tables.

These tables are designed to make it easy to complete the application form and show the cost of any particular loan over your preferred repayment period, either with or without the optional Personal Loan Protector cover.

Loans are available for a minimum of £200 and upwards in multiples of £50 up to £1,000 and in multiples of £100 thereafter. For each loan amount given in the tables the total amount payable, the monthly repayments and the Personal Loan Protector premium is given to show you exactly what your loan will cost.

Here's how.

1. In Row A, find the sum you wish to borrow for the term of repayment you require.

2. Row B will show you the total amount you will be paying, including the Personal Loan Protector premium (if applicable), interest, and arrangement fee of 1% of the sum you wish to borrow debited to your current account when your loan is set up.

3. Row C shows the Personal Loan Protector premium which will be added to the sum you wish to borrow and repaid over the period you choose.

4. Row D tells you the monthly instalment needed to repay the loan (including the Personal Loan Protector premium if applicable) and interest. Where the total amount repayable is not exactly divisible by the number of monthly repayments, a small adjustment will be made to the final repayment.

For example, a loan of £750 over 24 months will cost a total of £953.10 (Row B). The insurance premium will be £38.00 (Row C) which is added to the loan and is included in the monthly repayments of £39.40 (Row D). The 1% arrangement fee of £7.50 is debited to your current account when your loan is set up.

If you do not wish to take advantage of the Personal Loan Protector cover simply use Rows B and D in the 'Without Protection' section of the tables.

Where a particular loan amount is not shown, the repayments can be calculated quite simply:

---

eg:

For a loan of £1,500 with Personal Loan Protector cover repayable over 24 months

Repayments for a loan of £1,000 = £52.55 +
Repayments for a loan of £500 = £26.25
to give monthly repayments of £78.80

Similarly, repayments for a loan of £2,300 can be calculated by adding the repayments for a loan of £2,000 to those for a loan of £300.

Written quotations are available on request if required from any of our branches who will also be happy to answer any further queries you may have.

A Amount of Loan £	**200**	**250**	**300**	**350**	**400**	**450**	**500**	**550**	**600**	**650**	**700**
REPAYMENT TERM 12 MONTHS AT 10% p.a. flat										☐	With Personal Loan Protector
B Total Payable £	229.70	287.40	344.00	401.70	459.40	517.10	574.80	631.40	689.10	746.80	804.50
C Insurance Premium £	7.00	9.00	10.00	12.00	14.00	16.00	18.00	19.00	21.00	23.00	25.00
D Monthly Repayment £	18.98	23.74	28.42	33.18	37.95	42.72	47.48	52.16	56.93	61.69	66.46
B Total Payable £	222.00	277.50	333.00	388.50	444.00	499.50	555.00	610.50	666.00	721.50	777.00
D Monthly Repayment £	18.33	22.92	27.50	32.08	36.67	41.25	45.83	50.42	55.00	59.58	64.17
REPAYMENT TERM 18 MONTHS AT 10% p.a. flat										☐	With Personal Loan Protector
B Total Payable £	241.20	301.50	361.80	422.10	482.40	542.70	604.15	664.45	724.75	785.05	845.35
C Insurance Premium £	8.00	10.00	12.00	14.00	16.00	18.00	2[illegible].00	23.00	25.00	27.00	29.00
D Monthly Repayment £	13.29	16.61	19.93	23.26	26.58	29.90	33.29	36.61	39.93	43.25	46.58
B Total Payable £	232.00	290.00	348.00	406.00	464.00	522.00	580.00	638.00	696.00	754.00	812.00
D Monthly Repayment £	12.78	15.97	19.17	22.36	25.56	28.75	3[illegible].94	35.14	38.33	41.53	44.72
REPAYMENT TERM 24 MONTHS AT 10% p.a. flat										☐	With Personal Loan Protector
B Total Payable £	254.00	316.90	381.00	443.90	508.00	570.90	635.00	699.10	762.00	826.10	889.00
C Insurance Premium £	10.00	12.00	15.00	17.00	20.00	22.00	25.00	28.00	30.00	33.00	35.00
D Monthly Repayment £	10.50	13.10	15.75	18.35	21.00	23.60	26.25	28.90	31.50	34.15	36.75
B Total Payable £	242.00	302.50	363.00	423.50	484.00	544.50	605.00	665.50	726.00	786.50	847.00
D Monthly Repayment £	10.00	12.50	15.00	17.50	20.00	22.50	25.00	27.50	30.00	32.50	35.00
REPAYMENT TERM 30 MONTHS AT 10% p.a. flat										☐	With Personal Loan Protector
B Total Payable £	265.75	332.50	399.25	466.00	532.75	599.50	666.25	733.00	799.75	866.50	933.25
C Insurance Premium £	11.00	14.00	17.00	20.00	23.00	26.00	29.00	32.00	35.00	38.00	41.00
D Monthly Repayment £	8.79	11.00	13.21	15.42	17.63	19.83	22.04	24.25	26.46	28.67	30.88
B Total Payable £	252.00	315.00	378.00	441.00	504.00	567.00	630.00	693.00	756.00	819.00	882.00
D Monthly Repayment £	8.33	10.42	12.50	14.58	16.67	18.75	20.83	22.92	25.00	27.08	29.17
REPAYMENT TERM 36 MONTHS AT 10% p.a. flat										☐	With Personal Loan Protector
B Total Payable £	278.90	348.30	419.00	488.40	557.80	628.50	697.90	767.30	838.00	907.40	976.80
C Insurance Premium £	13.00	16.00	20.00	23.00	26.00	30.00	33.00	36.00	40.00	43.00	46.00
D Monthly Repayment £	7.69	9.61	11.56	13.47	15.38	17.33	19.25	21.16	23.11	25.03	26.94
B Total Payable £	262.00	327.50	393.00	458.50	524.00	589.50	655.00	720.50	786.00	851.50	917.00
D Monthly Repayment £	7.22	9.03	10.83	12.64	14.44	16.25	18.06	19.86	21.67	23.47	25.28
REPAYMENT TERM 48 MONTHS AT 11% p.a. flat										☐	With Personal Loan Protector
B Total Payable £	314.48	392.74	471.00	550.70	628.96	707.22	786.92	865.18	943.44	1,021.70	1,101.40
C Insurance Premium £	17.00	21.00	25.00	30.00	34.00	38.00	43.00	47.00	51.00	55.00	60.00
D Monthly Repayment £	6.51	8.13	9.75	11.40	13.02	14.64	16.29	17.91	19.53	21.15	22.80
B Total Payable £	290.00	362.50	435.00	507.50	580.00	652.50	725.00	797.50	870.00	942.50	1,015.00
D Monthly Repayment £	6.00	7.50	9.00	10.50	12.00	13.50	15.00	16.50	18.00	19.50	21.00
REPAYMENT TERM 60 MONTHS AT 11% p.a. flat										☐	With Personal Loan Protector
B Total Payable £	344.55	430.30	516.05	603.35	689.10	774.85	862.15	947.90	1,033.65	1,119.40	1,206.70
C Insurance Premium £	21.00	26.00	31.00	37.00	42.00	47.00	53.00	58.00	63.00	68.00	74.00
D Monthly Repayment £	5.71	7.13	8.55	10.00	11.42	12.84	14.29	15.71	17.13	18.55	20.00
B Total Payable £	312.00	390.00	468.00	546.00	624.00	702.00	780.00	858.00	936.00	1,014.00	1,092.00
D Monthly Repayment £	5.17	6.46	7.75	9.04	10.33	11.63	12.92	14.21	15.50	16.79	18.08
A Amount of Loan £	**200**	**250**	**300**	**350**	**400**	**450**	**500**	**550**	**600**	**650**	**700**

750	800	850	900	950	1,000	1,100	2,000	2,100	3,000	3,100	4,000	4,100	5,000
(APR* 21·7%)			☐ Without Protection **(APR* 21·8%)**										
862.20	918.80	976.50	1,034.20	1,091.90	1,149.60	1,263.90	2,299.20	2,413.50	3,448.80	3,563.10	4,598.40	4,712.70	5,748.00
27.00	28.00	30.00	32.00	34.00	36.00	39.00	72.00	75.00	108.00	111.00	144.00	147.00	180.00
71.23	75.90	80.67	85.43	90.20	94.97	104.41	189.93	199.38	284.90	294.34	379.87	389.31	474.83
832.50	888.00	943.50	999.00	1,054.50	1,110.00	1,221.00	2,220.00	2,331.00	3,330.00	3,441.00	4,440.00	4,551.00	5,550.00
68.75	73.33	77.92	82.50	87.08	91.67	100.83	183.33	192.50	275.00	284.17	366.67	375.83	458.33
(APR* 21·3%)			☐ Without Protection **(APR* 21·3%)**										
905.65	965.95	1,026.25	1,086.55	1,146.85	1,208.30	1,328.90	2,416.60	2,537.20	3,624.90	3,745.50	4,833.20	4,953.80	6,041.50
31.00	33.00	35.00	37.00	39.00	42.00	46.00	84.00	88.00	126.00	130.00	168.00	172.00	210.00
49.90	53.22	56.54	59.86	63.19	66.57	73.22	133.14	139.79	199.72	206.36	266.29	272.93	332.86
870.00	928.00	986.00	1,044.00	1,102.00	1,160.00	1,276.00	2,320.00	2,436.00	3,480.00	3,596.00	4,640.00	4,756.00	5,800.00
47.92	51.11	54.31	57.50	60.69	63.89	70.28	127.78	134.17	191.67	198.06	255.56	261.94	319.44
(APR* 20·9%)			☐ Without Protection **(APR* 20·9%)**										
953.10	1,016.00	1,080.10	1,143.00	1,207.10	1,271.20	1,398.20	2,542.40	2,669.40	3,813.60	3,940.60	5,084.80	5,211.80	6,356.00
38.00	40.00	43.00	45.00	48.00	51.00	56.00	102.00	107.00	153.00	158.00	204.00	209.00	255.00
39.40	42.00	44.65	47.25	49.90	52.55	57.80	105.10	110.35	157.65	162.90	210.20	215.45	262.75
907.50	968.00	1,028.50	1,089.00	1,149.50	1,210.00	1,331.00	2,420.00	2,541.00	3,630.00	3,751.00	4,840.00	4,961.00	6,050.00
37.50	40.00	42.50	45.00	47.50	50.00	55.00	100.00	105.00	150.00	155.00	200.00	205.00	250.00
(APR* 20·5%)			☐ Without Protection **(APR* 20·6%)**										
1,000.00	1,066.75	1,133.50	1,200.25	1,267.00	1,333.75	1,466.00	2,667.50	2,799.75	4,001.25	4,133.50	5,335.00	5,467.25	6,668.75
44.00	47.00	50.00	53.00	56.00	59.00	64.00	118.00	123.00	177.00	182.00	236.00	241.00	295.00
33.08	35.29	37.50	39.71	41.92	44.13	48.50	88.25	92.63	132.38	136.75	176.50	180.88	220.63
945.00	1,008.00	1,071.00	1,134.00	1,197.00	1,260.00	1,386.00	2,520.00	2,646.00	3,780.00	3,906.00	5,040.00	5,166.00	6,300.00
31.25	33.33	35.42	37.50	39.58	41.67	45.83	83.33	87.50	125.00	129.17	166.67	170.83	208.33
(APR* 20·2%)			☐ Without Protection **(APR* 20·3%)**										
1,047.50	1,116.90	1,186.30	1,257.00	1,326.40	1,397.10	1,535.90	2,794.20	2,933.00	4,191.30	4,330.10	5,588.40	5,727.20	6,985.50
50.00	53.00	56.00	60.00	63.00	67.00	73.00	134.00	140.00	201.00	207.00	268.00	274.00	335.00
28.89	30.80	32.72	34.67	36.58	38.53	42.36	77.06	80.89	115.59	119.42	154.12	157.95	192.65
982.50	1,048.00	1,113.50	1,179.00	1,244.50	1,310.00	1,441.00	2,620.00	2,751.00	3,930.00	4,061.00	5,240.00	5,371.00	6,550.00
27.08	28.89	30.69	32.50	34.31	36.11	39.72	72.22	75.83	108.33	111.94	144.44	148.06	180.56
(APR* 21·5%)			☐ Without Protection **(APR* 21·6%)**										
1,179.66	1,257.92	1,337.62	1,415.88	1,494.14	1,573.84	1,730.36	3,147.68	3,304.20	4,721.52	4,878.04	6,295.36	6,451.88	7,869.20
64.00	68.00	73.00	77.00	81.00	86.00	94.00	172.00	180.00	258.00	266.00	344.00	352.00	430.00
24.42	26.04	27.69	29.31	30.93	32.58	35.82	65.16	68.40	97.74	100.98	130.32	133.56	162.90
1,087.50	1,160.00	1,232.50	1,305.00	1,377.50	1,450.00	1,595.00	2,900.00	3,045.00	4,350.00	4,495.00	5,800.00	5,945.00	7,250.00
22.50	24.00	25.50	27.00	28.50	30.00	33.00	60.00	63.00	90.00	93.00	120.00	123.00	150.00
(APR* 21·0%)			☐ Without Protection **(APR* 21·0%)**										
1,292.45	1,378.20	1,465.50	1,551.25	1,637.00	1,724.30	1,895.80	3,448.60	3,620.10	5,172.90	5,344.40	6,897.20	7,068.70	8,621.50
79.00	84.00	90.00	95.00	100.00	106.00	116.00	212.00	222.00	318.00	328.00	424.00	434.00	530.00
21.42	22.84	24.28	25.70	27.13	28.57	31.41	57.14	59.99	85.72	88.56	114.29	117.13	142.86
1,170.00	1,248.00	1,326.00	1,404.00	1,482.00	1,560.00	1,716.00	3,120.00	3,276.00	4,680.00	4,836.00	6,240.00	6,396.00	7,800.00
19.38	20.67	21.96	23.25	24.54	25.83	28.42	51.67	54.25	77.50	80.08	103.33	105.92	129.17
750	**800**	**850**	**900**	**950**	**1,000**	**1,100**	**2,000**	**2,100**	**3,000**	**3,100**	**4,000**	**4,100**	**5,000**

List of Tape Extracts

1 'Good Afternoon, Mr Phillips' (1.6)
2 Pin Men (2.1)
3 Radio Magazine Programme (EE2)
4 Elvis (3.3)
5 Digging for Facts (3.4)
6 Tiny, Tumbledown, Overpriced & Co. (3.5)
7 Angry, Sad, Happy Sarcastic . . . (3.6)
8 Declan's Problems (3.8)
9 Careers Counsellor (4.2)
10 Asking for a Bank Loan A (4.3)
11 Asking for a Bank Loan B (4.4)
12 Gobbledegook (4.5)
13 Making a Phone Call A (5.1)
14 Making a Phone Call B (5.1)
15 'This is a Machine Talking' (5.3)
16 'Will That Be All Right, Mum?' (5.4)
17 Phone Tactics A (5.5)
18 Phone Tactics B (5.5)
19 Answering the Phone (5.8)
20 Barsetshire Technical College (5.10)
21 More Difficult Calls A (5.11)
22 More Difficult Calls B (5.11)
23 More Difficult Calls C (5.11)
24 A Morning at Planetts (6.3)
25 The Mugging (6.5)
26 Gilbert's Fashions (6.6)
27 Witness in Court (6.8)
28 ALF – the Ford Cortina (7.2)
29 Dealing with Awkward Situations (7.7)
30 'It was the Buses' (8.2)
31 Tricks in Argument (9.1)
32 Coping with Insults (9.3)

Skills List

1 Using Your Voice

a) Pronounce words clearly, with distinct articulation.	1.1; 1.2; EE1
b) Spell out unusual or difficult words clearly, using alphabetical code if necessary.	1.3; 1.4
c) Exercise the mouth and voice to improve articulation, audibility and control.	1.5
d) Identify tones of voice appropriate to various situations.	1.6; EE1
e) Use a tone of voice appropriate to a particular situation and audience.	1.7; 1.8; 1.9; EE1
f) Use your voice to convey your feelings accurately.	1.8; EE1
g) Use the techniques of pause, stress, variety in pace, volume and pitch to produce interest in your voice.	1.9; 1.10; EE1

2 Instructions and Explanations

a) Describe pictures, diagrams and objects clearly and accurately.	2.2; 2.3; EE2
b) Give easily followed travel directions using a street map and transport map.	2.4
c) Give instructions and explanations in clear and logically ordered steps.	2.4; 2.5; 2.6; 2.7; EE2
d) Adopt an appropriate tone and vocabulary in instructions and explanations to suit a particular audience and occasion.	2.5; 2.6; 2.7; EE2
e) Use comparisons, analogies and landmarks to help people remember your instructions.	2.4; 2.5; 2.7; EE2
f) Use diagrams, charts and other visual (or audio-visual) aids to illustrate instructions and explanations.	2.6; 2.7; EE2
g) Use practical demonstration to help in giving instructions and explanations.	2.7; 2.8; 2.9

3 Listening

a) Listen carefully to a message and relay it accurately.	3.2
b) Listen carefully to what people say in order to obtain information.	3.3; 3.4
c) Listen carefully to what customers and clients say and extract the facts needed to help them.	3.5; EE3
d) Identify the tone of voice of a speaker and appreciate its importance in interpreting what s/he is saying and feeling.	3.5; 3.6; 3.8; EE3
e) Identify the contribution of body language to what is being said.	3.7; 3.8; EE3
f) Listen sympathetically to problems and difficulties and give support both verbally and through appropriate tone of voice, gestures, expression etc.	3.8
g) Listen with an open mind without allowing appearance, accent, dress etc. to interfere irrelevantly with the communication.	EE3

4 Help and Advice

a) Identify appropriate tone in asking for help and advice.	4.2; 4.3; 4.4; EE4
b) Use effective techniques to obtain help and advice from an expert.	4.2; 4.3; 4.4; EE4
c) Ask for simplification of complex ideas, vocabulary, jargon etc.	4.4; 4.5; 4.6
d) Relay complex information in a simplified form suitable for a non-expert listener.	4.6; 4.8
e) Give advice in a clear, tactful and well organised form.	4.7; 4.8; 4.9; EE4

5 Using the Telephone

a) Identify the reasons for phone calls failing to achieve their purpose.	5.1; 5.5
b) Prepare notes to help in making an efficient phone call.	5.2; 5.3; EE5
c) Cope confidently with an answering machine.	5.3; EE5
d) Use a tone of voice appropriate to convey a message accurately and tactfully over the phone especially in difficult situations.	5.4; 5.6; EE5

e) Answer the phone helpfully and efficiently.	5.8; 5.9; 5.10; EE5
f) Obtain information from a caller in a friendly and methodical manner and record it accurately.	5.9; 5.10; EE5
g) Cope effectively with difficult callers.	5.10; 5.11
h) Cope effectively with bad lines etc.	5.11

6 Reporting

a) Give an account of an event or series of events in a logical sequence.	6.1; 6.2; 6.3; 6.7; 6.8; EE6
b) Edit information so that only what is relevant is relayed and priority is given to important items.	6.1; 6.2; 6.3; 6.7; 6.8; EE6
c) Distinguish between facts and personal opinions when giving an account.	6.4; 6.7; 6.8; EE6
d) Identify and use an appropriate tone, formal or informal, humorous or serious, to suit a particular audience for an oral report.	6.3; 6.4; 6.5; 6.6; 6.7; 6.8; EE6
e) Prepare a report for a formal occasion.	6.8

7 Making an Impression

a) Persuade people of the benefits of various goods and services.	7.1; 7.2; EE7
b) Present goods and services as positively as possible.	7.3; 7.8; EE7
c) Help a customer by identifying what s/he needs and wants.	7.4; 7.8; EE7
d) Persuade others to accept your judgements.	7.4; 7.5; EE7
e) Advertise a service or product.	7.6
f) Deal with awkward encounters.	7.7
g) Identify and put into practice techniques for coping effectively with being interviewed.	7.8; 7.9; EE7
h) Conduct an effective interview.	7.7
i) Present yourself and the skills you can offer in a positive and attractive way to others.	EE7

8 Putting Your Case

a) Analyse a case and break it down into arguable points.	8.1; 8.3; 8.5; EE8
b) Put the points of an argument in an order of priority appropriate to the occasion, the audience and your aims.	8.1; 8.4; 8.5; EE8
c) Identify and use the most effective approach to persuade a particular audience.	8.2; 8.4; 8.5; 8.8; EE8
d) Make a complaint effectively.	8.5
e) Distinguish between fact and opinion in formulating arguments.	8.6; EE8
f) Use supporting evidence to strengthen arguments.	8.7; EE8

9 Under Discussion

a) Identify tricks and false reasoning in other people's arguments.	9.1; 9.2; EE9
b) Identify and cope with insults and personal remarks introduced into a discussion.	9.2; 9.3; 9.4; EE9
c) Identify and cope with prejudiced statements and attitudes.	9.4; EE9
d) Look for the other side of an argument.	9.5; 9.6; EE9
e) Discuss issues constructively with people holding opposing, possibly uncongenial attitudes.	9.4; 9.5; 9.6; EE9
f) Argue affectively against an opponent's case.	9.4; 9.5; 9.6; EE9
g) Maintain the momentum of a discussion.	9.6; EE9
h) Use factual evidence persuasively.	9.6; EE9

Extended Exercise Assessment Guide

This guide indicates which skills from the index on pp. 119–122 may be tested by each of the nine Extended Exercises.

EE1 – Bits and Pieces
1a) e) f) g)

EE2 – Radio Magazine
1e) g)
2a) c) d) e) f) g)
4c) d)

EE3 – Seagull Retreat
1b) e)
3c) d) e) g)
7c)

EE4 – Phone-in: The Parent Problem
1d) e)
2c) d) g)
3c) d) f) g)
4a) b) e)
7c) d)

EE5 – Round-Britain Tour
1a) c) e) f)
3a) c)
5b) c) d) e) f)

EE6 – Holiday 2000
1e) f) g)
2b) e)
6a) b) c) d)

EE7 – Odd Job Agency
1e)
3c) d)
7a) b) c) d)

EE8 – Putting Your Case
1a) e) f) g)
7a)
8a) b) c) e) f)

EE9 – WCC versus BRAG and Others
1e) f) g)
2c) d) e) g)
3b) d) e) g)
7a) b) d) g) h)
9a) b) c) d) e) f) g) h)

Acknowledgments

For permission to reproduce copyright material the authors and publishers wish to thank the following: extracts (pp. 1–2) from *The Puffin Book of Tongue Twisters*, © Lutterworth Press; photo (p. 6) © Brian Gunn, reprinted by kind permission of the National Anti-Vivisection Society Ltd; jokes (pp. 8–10) from *The Ha-Ha Bonk Book* by Janet and Allen Ahlberg (Kestrel Books, 1982), © Allen Ahlberg, 1982, reprinted by permission of Penguin Books Ltd; jokes (pp. 8–10) from *The Crack-a-Joke Book* (Oxfam); extract (p. 15) from the *A–Z Atlas of London* (Geographers' A–Z Map Co. Ltd) based on maps produced by the Ordnance Survey and reproduced here with the permission of the Controller of Her Majesty's Stationery Office, Crown Copyright reserved; map (p. 16): London Regional Transport Underground Map (registered user No. 85/E/293); extracts (pp. 18–19) from *The Highway Code* with permission of the Controller of Her Majesty's Stationery Office, Crown Copyright reserved; dartboard drawing (p. 20) by Ruth Boothby; articles (pp. 36–37) from *New Scientist*, 28 February 1985; Factsheet on Police Questioning (p. 40): *Know Your Rights Factsheets*, © National Council of Civil Liberties 1982; extracts (pp. 41–45) from *Why Stop Smoking?*, *Can you Avoid Cancer?*, *Looking After Yourself* and *That's the Limit* all reproduced by permission of the Health Education Council, London; photo (p. 67) © Frederick Jackson, supplied by the National Youth Bureau; 'What the Law says about buying things' (pp. 86–7) from *How to Put Things Right* published by the Office of Fair Trading; extract (p. 91) from *How Girls Learn to be Women* by Sue Sharpe (Penguin Books, 1976), © Sue Sharpe 1976, reprinted by permission of Penguin Books Ltd extracts (p. 92) from *Things We Do* written by W. Murray and illustrated by J. H. Wingfield, reproduced by permission of Ladybird Books Ltd; extract (p. 93) from *Girls and Boys: The Limits of Non-Sexist Childrearing* by Sara Stein (Chatto and Windus, 1984), reproduced by permission of Chatto and Windus; publicity leaflets (pp. 100–101) reprinted by permission of the Down's Children's Association.

Every effort has been made to trace copyright holders of material reproduced in this book. Any rights not acknowledged here will be acknowledged in subsequent printings if notice is given to the publisher.